ESOPs and Corporate Governance
A guide for directors and fiduciaries

Third Edition

ESOPs and Corporate Governance
A guide for directors and fiduciaries
Third Edition

Merri Ash
Kelly Q. Driscoll
Michael Falk
Colleen Helmer
Brian Ippensen
Alex W. Kirby
Anthony Mathews
Helen Morrison
Corey Rosen
James Steiker
Cecil Ursprung

The National Center for Employee Ownership
Oakland, California

This publication is designed to provide accurate and authoritative information in regard to the subject matter covered. It is sold with the understanding that the publisher is not engaged in rendering legal, accounting, or other professional service. If legal advice or other expert assistance is required, the services of a competent professional person should be sought.

Legal, accounting, and other rules affecting business often change. Before making decisions based on the information you find here or in any publication from any publisher, you should ascertain what changes might have occurred and what changes might be forthcoming. The NCEO's Web site (including the members-only area) and newsletter for members provide regular updates on these changes. If you have any questions or concerns about a particular issue, check with your professional advisor or, if you are an NCEO member, call or email us.

ESOPs and Corporate Governance, 3rd ed.

Book design by Scott Rodrick

Copyright © 2004, 2009 by The National Center for Employee Ownership. All rights reserved. No part of this book may be reproduced or transmitted in any form or by any means, electronic or mechanical, including photocopying, recording, or by any information storage and retrieval system, without prior written permission from the publisher.

ISBN-10: 1-932924-65-5
ISBN-13: 978-1-932924-65-7

First edition, 2004; second edition, 2007; third edition, 2009

The National Center for Employee Ownership
1736 Franklin St., 8th Flr.
Oakland, CA 94612
(510) 208-1300
Fax (510) 272-9510
www.nceo.org

Contents

Introduction **vii**
Corey Rosen

1. ESOP Governance Q&A **1**
   Corey Rosen

2. ESOP Participants and Shareholder Rights
   James Steiker **19**

3. Shareholder Obligations of the ESOP Trustee
   Brian Ippensen and Merri Ash **29**

4. A Practical Guide for Company Stock Fiduciaries
   Kelly Q. Driscoll and Alex W. Kirby **37**

5. Who Should Be the Fiduciary?
   Corey Rosen **55**

6. Notes to In-House Employee Fiduciaries
   Anthony Mathews **61**

7. Don't Be Fooled: Sarbanes-Oxley Applies to Private ESOP Companies
   Helen Morrison, Colleen Helmer, and Michael Falk **69**

8. ESOP Corporate Governance in a New Era
   Helen Morrison **81**

9. The Role of the Board in ESOP Companies   **97**
   Cecil Ursprung

   About the Authors   **107**

   About the NCEO   **111**

Introduction
Corey Rosen

In recent years, corporate governance has moved to center stage in discussions about American business. While most of this discussion has focused on large publicly traded companies, the concerns raised about how companies are governed apply to all companies. Responsible governance practices can be a check on abusive and even illegal management practices, but they play an even more important role in the more mundane affairs of a business. An effective board can help generate new ideas, caution against excessively risky ventures, assure that management its doing its job well, provide credibility and contacts with customers and suppliers, and inspire confidence among employees. For ESOP companies, additional governance issues are raised both by law and by a greater ethical and practical responsibility to employees. ESOP trustees must act to protect the interests of plan participants, even if this sometimes conflicts with management. Employees often raise questions and concerns about governance that, if not answered in a compelling way, can create cynicism and distrust.

This book was written to help ESOP companies think through their governance issues. An important part of the book is a survey on governance practices in ESOP companies. It provides details on board compensation and composition, trustee selection and responsibilities, and employee roles on boards. Other chapters deal with how to select an ESOP trustee, legal obligations of the trustee under ERISA and as a shareholder, best practices for ESOP boards (with a particular eye to concepts established by the Sarbanes-Oxley Act, which only legally affects publicly traded companies), issues when employees are fiduciaries, the role of the board, and special legal considerations for the governance of ESOP companies.

The authors of the chapters in the book are all leading experts in the field. We very much appreciate their input and support for this project. We welcome your comments.

The third edition of this book includes various revisions to chapter 2; minor changes to chapters 1, 6, 7, 8, and 9; and updates to the author biographies.

CHAPTER ONE

ESOP Governance Q&A
Corey Rosen

The issues covered in this Q&A are covered in more detail in other chapters in this book. This chapter, however, can be used as a quick reference tool or overview of corporate governance topics.

Voting ESOP Shares

Who actually votes the ESOP shares?

The plan's trustee generally votes all of the shares in the ESOP, whether allocated or not. The plan document indicates how the trustee must decide how to vote. In closely held companies, the trustee must follow participant directions on allocated shares on several major corporate issues (sale, liquidation, sale of all or substantially all the assets, recapitalization, merger, and related issues) but does not have to solicit instructions on voting for the board, agreeing to tender the stock, or selling the stock, among other issues. In publicly traded companies, trustees must follow participant directions on allocated shares on all issues presented for a shareholder vote. Otherwise, the trustee usually follows the directions of management, the plan committee, or another fiduciary specified in the plan. While this usually causes no problems, the trustee, or the person(s) directing the trustee, still must act in the best interests of plan participants. Note that while the law requires trustees to solicit employee instructions on specified issues, the trustee has

1

a higher legal obligation under ERISA to override these instructions if they are contrary to the law or plan documents. Such actions are very rare and need compelling justification, however.

How is it decided who elects the board of an ESOP company?

In a publicly traded company, the board of directors is elected by all shareholders and is responsible for the hiring and firing of management. Employees in a public company ESOP can vote their allocated shares just like any other shareholder. In some public companies, they can direct the voting of unallocated shares as well. In practice, however, employees rarely use the vote any more actively than do other individual shareholders, meaning an ESOP has little or no impact on day-to-day operations of the company or the composition of its board.

In a closely held company, there is more variation. In the most common scenario, employees have only limited voting rights (see the question "Who actually votes the ESOP shares?" in this chapter as well as the chapter on "ESOP Corporate Governance in a New Era"), and do not vote for the board. Instead, the trustee exercises voting rights. Typically, the board of directors selects the trustee, who can be anyone but is usually either a corporate officer or, in larger companies, an outsider such as a bank. The trustee, in turn, votes the ESOP shares for the election of the board. Usually, the trustee acts according to directions from the ESOP committee (see the section "ESOP Administrative Committees" in this chapter for details on how they function), although in some companies, the functions of the committee and the trustee are joined in a board of trustees. The committee is usually appointed by the board and is made up of company officers. This circular arrangement means, in effect, that management and/or the board (these are often the same) controls the company in much the same way it did before the ESOP. Of course, whoever acts as an ESOP's fiduciary (that is, whoever makes decisions for the plan) is legally responsible to make those decisions in the best interests of plan participants.

While companies have the discretion to set up the plan this way, some plans provide for greater employee involvement. For instance, nonmanagement employees may be represented on the ESOP committee.

Employees may be given full voting rights on their shares. Employees may also elect one or more representatives to the board. Companies have found that this higher level of employee involvement is usually a plus for the company and rarely results in significant policy changes other than ones on which there is consensus among the managers as well.

The law requires employees to be able to vote on "recapitalizations." What does this mean?

Recapitalization is defined by state corporate statutes, so it can vary from state to state. Generally, it means a change in the number of authorized shares or in the relative rights and preferences of those shares. A small increase in the number of shares may not qualify as a recapitalization. Similarly, many companies already have authorized but unissued shares they can use for various financing purposes such as selling an ownership stake to an investor or making contributions to the ESOP. Going public may often be a recapitalization, but refinancing loans would generally not be. If the state statutes require that shareholders be able to vote on an issue as a recapitalization issue, the vote on this must be passed through to ESOP participants.

When do employees get to vote on selling a company?

The sale of a company does not necessarily require an employee vote. The sale of the assets of a company does, but the sale of stock generally would not, and certainly would not if the company's stock were exchanged for stock in an acquiring firm, other than through a merger. State law would define whether a sale requires a shareholder vote, in which case the vote would be passed through to employees.

Aside from the legally required minimum, can employees direct the trustee as to the voting or tendering of the shares held in their accounts in regard to acquisition proposals?

The law here is very unsettled. Many public companies, and some private firms, provide that employees can direct the ESOP trustee to vote or tender their allocated shares as directed and their unallocated or undirected shares in the same proportion as the allocated shares. Generally, companies that do this name each participant as a fiduciary for the ESOP shares. The issue here is whether the trustee can simply record the votes or directions or must make an independent judgment. The consensus of legal opinion on this issue seems to be that employees can direct allocated shares, can be named as fiduciaries for all shares (by designating a pro-rata portion of unallocated shares to each employee), and can give directions to the trustee. The trustee, however, should ultimately have the power to make an independent decision if there is, as the Department of Labor puts it, a compelling reason to override the employee directions, such as persuasive evidence that both short- and long-term stock values will do better under an offer the employees do not favor. In more ambiguous situations, however, employee directions would probably be acceptable.

In any case, the trustees must create a clear paper trail showing why the decision was made and why it is consistent with ERISA. Participants must also be given clear, objective information about the competing alternatives, much as any other shareholder would be in a proxy battle. Their vote must be confidential. It is also possible that decisions regarding tendering or sale of securities will be subject to state and/or federal securities rules. Companies should check with counsel to make sure that any votes are in compliance with these requirements.

Can ESOPs be structured so employees vote other than one share/one vote?

There are two ways to do this. First, in closely held companies, the law allows an ESOP to pass through voting on a one-person, one-vote basis. In some cases, however, other voting arrangements are desired, such as giving some employees more votes than others in a manner unrelated to their share ownership. On legally required pass-through issues (all issues in public companies; a limited number of issues in closely held companies), employees must either be allowed to vote their allocated shares according to how many they own or get one vote each. For unallocated shares, or for issues for which there is no required pass-through, the trustee can be directed to vote the shares in whatever way the plan is written to dictate. For instance, a company might hold an employee vote allowing all employees (participants in the plan or not) the right to vote. The trustee would then vote the ESOP shares in the same manner, either proportionately or "winner take all."

The ESOP and the ESOP Trustee as Shareholder

Does the ESOP trustee have the same standing as other shareholders?

Yes.

What are the basic shareholder rights for an ESOP trustee?

These vary by state but generally include the right to a notice of meetings (one shareholder meeting per year is usually the legal minimum); the right to call special meetings, which applies only to those who meet minimum ownership thresholds (usually 20%); the right to inspect a list of other shareholders; the right to vote for the election and removal of directors; and the right to vote on the adoption, amendment, or repeal of bylaws or articles of incorporation, mergers or consolidations, share exchanges, division of the company, sales of all or substantially all the assets, dissolutions, or conversions to another corporate status. Trustee shareholders must also receive annual financial statements; full and fair disclosure in acquisitions; payment of fair value for shares if there is special treatment for one class of owners, or when the company is sold or merged; and, in some states, additional rights to prevent takeovers.

Do ESOP trustee shareholder rights add to ERISA responsibilities?

ERISA normally overrides state law where there is a conflict. Shareholder rights arguably increase the trustee's responsibilities under ERISA, however. For instance, the trustee must negotiate for the best price for the ESOP under ERISA rules; shareholder rights assure that the trustee can get all the information needed to do so. In an acquisition, shareholder rights provide additional ammunition to trustees to protect and promote participant interests. Where fundamental changes in company structure could adversely affect participants, shareholder dissenter and litigation rights help the trustee assure the ESOP is treated fairly. The Department of Labor has argued that trustees should go one step further, using shareholder rights affirmatively to assure, among other things, competent, independent boards; good employee-relations practices; and sound long-term strategy. This more aggressive view has not been tested in court, although it seems clear that a trustee would have the right to take these actions as a shareholder. Note also that ESOP companies may designate another fiduciary to exercise shareholder rights.

What is the role of the trustee with respect to executive and board compensation?

This is one of the most potentially controversial issues in an ESOP. Case law—and good practice—suggest that the following guidelines need to be followed:

1. Executive and board pay should be reasonable. It should be justifiable in terms of what similar companies pay for people with similar responsibilities and contributions to the company. Excessive executive and board pay in an ESOP company not only gives rise to ordinary "wasting of corporate asset" issues, but also to issues of whether the ESOP overpaid for the stock (because future profits were drained off for unreasonable pay).
2. The trustee and the board should be able to document that they have given careful and proper consideration to determining executive pay, including, if needed, survey data from industry or other sources or the use of a qualified compensation consultant.
3. Closely held companies may want to model the governance practices that securities laws require public companies to follow with regard to executive and board pay. For instance, having an independent compensation committee can help protect against possible lawsuits and help assure plan participants that the plan is being run properly.

Despite these concerns, it is important to note that legal problems concerning executive and board pay have been rare in ESOP companies.

The ESOP Fiduciary and the ESOP Trustee

What is an ESOP trustee?

The ESOP trustee is the person or institution that normally has the formal responsibility to make sure the plan is operated for "the exclusive benefit of plan participants." Trustees can be "independent" or "directed." An independent trustee makes decisions for the plan based on its own judgment, relying as needed on advice from qualified professionals; a directed trustee takes directions from another party, which could be the ESOP committee, management, or employee participants (such as employees directing the voting of their allocated shares). Directed trustees have very limited fiduciary responsibility, as explained below.

Is the ESOP trustee the same as the ESOP fiduciary?

In most cases, the trustee is the fiduciary, but the two functions are not necessarily the same. Plans must designate fiduciaries; they can designate them for all issues or have different fiduciaries for particular issues. A fiduciary is anyone who makes decisions about plan operations, including its management or the disposition of its assets. Fiduciaries can also be people who render investment advice for a fee. Thus, a directed trustee has a lessened fiduciary obligation if it is not making decisions. (Nonetheless, a directed trustee still must confirm that any directions received are consistent with the plan documents and ERISA; if they are not, the trustee should inform the fiduciary and make a decision that does fit these guidelines.) Similarly, if the plan document permits it, on any particular issue, the trustee may cede decision-making to or share the responsibility with someone else. It is important to recognize that even though someone may not be named as a fiduciary, that person could act in that role, and thus have a fiduciary's legal responsibility if he or she effectively makes a decision with regard to plan operations.

Who is a fiduciary?

A fiduciary is anyone who makes decisions for the plan, causes someone to make a decision about the plan, or, in some cases, advises someone making decisions about the plan. Put differently, it is anyone who exercises control over plan assets, directly or indirectly. Anyone (or any group of people) can be a fiduciary. Most commonly, it is a manager, a committee of management and/or employees, a bank trust department, or (rarely) an ESOP professional.

How does someone become a fiduciary?

The plan must designate a fiduciary. But the answer to the question "Who is a fiduciary?" is based on what a person actually does, regardless of what the plan says. So, for instance, if a CEO directs a plan trustee to take a certain action, even if the plan trustee is named as the fiduciary, for that decision, the CEO is the fiduciary.

What are fiduciary actions?

Anything that involves the management of plan assets is a fiduciary act, including, but not limited to, setting the stock price, voting shares, allocating responsibility for plan administration, selling stock, and interpreting plan provisions.

Can someone be a fiduciary for just one issue?

Yes.

What is a named fiduciary?

This is simply the individual or individuals (or the holder of a specific office such as the trusteeship) that the plan specifies as a fiduciary. Naming the fiduciary clarifies where the decision-making authority for the plan lies.

Who selects the fiduciary?

The board of directors typically selects the fiduciary, but the plan could provide that the ESOP committee, the employees, the existing trustee, or any other individual or group could select the fiduciary.

Is the plan sponsor automatically a fiduciary?

The plan sponsor is not automatically a fiduciary for the plan. The company, and its officers and board members, are fiduciaries only to the extent that they take actions that makes them fiduciaries. This can include selecting, directing, or influencing named fiduciaries to take actions concerning the plan's assets. For instance, if the board pressures a trustee to act a certain way, even if it does not specifically tell the trustee how to act, the plan sponsor and its officers and directors could be considered to have engaged in a fiduciary act. However, the establishment, termination, and amendment of plans are not in themselves fiduciary acts.

Does the board or management become a fiduciary or co-fiduciary simply by appointing a fiduciary?

This is an unresolved issue. Courts have generally said no, but in the Department of Labor's August 2003 lawsuit against Enron (which was still ongoing as of this writing), it asserted that the board and management did have fiduciary responsibility for Enron's stock ownership plans because they appointed, and had the right to change, fiduciaries for the plans.

In recent years, courts have also focused on the board's duty to monitor the fiduciary to make sure the fiduciary is qualified to do the job and is complying with ERISA and plan documents. This could be interpreted in a very broad way so that the board essentially becomes a co-fiduciary, but the courts have consistently taken a more narrow view that the board should be alert to obvious significant fiduciary failures but is not required to do detailed oversight. For instance, if fiduciaries are acting in ways where they show a clear personal conflict of interest detrimental to the plan, promote employee stock as an investment in a 401(k) or KSOP plan when they have information that indicates it is a poor investment, or fail to obtain necessary professional advice on valuations, this would fall under the failure-to-monitor rubric.

How does a fiduciary know if it is complying with the "exclusive benefit rule?"

ERISA requires that fiduciaries act for "the exclusive benefit" of plan participants. This obviously cannot mean what it literally says. Any action with respect to the ESOP that incidentally benefited the company or its other owners would be in violation of a literal reading of this rule.

As courts have interpreted it, however, the test is to look at where plan participant interests conflict or could conflict with the interests of the company, its other owners, or other parties. The fiduciary first has to decide whether the conflict of interests is one where his or her own self-interest is such that it would be impossible to discharge fiduciary duties in a manner that has "an eye single" to the benefit of participants. If such a conflict is an issue, then the fiduciary should not be involved in that decision. A fiduciary's decisions must be made based on an appropriate and, if needed, intensive investigation of the facts at hand, often with professional independent advice. Any decision must further the interests of plan participants as participants in a benefit plan (not necessarily as employees).

Can officers or managers of the company be held responsible for fiduciary failure if their business decisions about the company do not work out?

Decisions made about running the company are not fiduciary decisions for the ESOP, even though they affect ESOP asset values.

Can a fiduciary be held responsible for misrepresenting facts about the ESOP?

Yes. The fiduciary must provide employees with accurate information, orally and in writing. Misrepresentations of the plan that participants adversely rely on can lead to legal action.

In determining whether a fiduciary acted prudently, does the law look to the results of the decision or the process by which it was made?

The courts consistently look to how the decision was made. Was proper procedure followed to assure independent, expert advice? Were all relevant factors considered? Did the fiduciary act to protect plan interests, or to promote the interests of others? The fact that the decision yielded a negative result (such as the stock price declining) is not in itself proof that the process by which it was made was imprudent.

Does having an independent trustee insulate the company from fiduciary liability?

An independent trustee creates a stronger legal presumption that decisions were made to benefit plan participants, but the trustee still must be able to show that that is the case.

Does having an inside trustee lead to a stricter test for whether the trustee acted for the benefit of plan participants in any given decision?

The presence of an inside trustee, especially if there is a conflict of interest, can make it more difficult to prove that the trustee acted in the interests of plan participants. The trustee will be subject to a higher standard of proof that his or her decisions are proper than an independent, qualified outsider would be.

If a fiduciary or trustee makes a decision based on the advice of a qualified professional advisor, will this provide protection against legal action?

While a fiduciary or trustee must seek qualified professional advice on a number of issues relating to the ESOP, this in not, in itself, enough to avoid fiduciary responsibility. The fiduciary or trustee must independently investigate whether the advice is appropriate. This is especially the case if there is a potential conflict between the trustee or fiduciary and the ESOP's best interests.

Is a fiduciary required to fix a problem created by a predecessor?

Yes. A fiduciary does have a responsibility to repair any problems created by a predecessor.

How is a loss to an ESOP that was caused by a breach of fiduciary duties measured?

The ESOP must have restored to it the amount of money that it would have had if the breach had not occurred. For instance, if the ESOP paid too much for shares, then the difference must be restored, either in cash (with interest) or additional shares. If the loss is not monetary, such as a failure to apply proper vesting schedules before anyone has received a payout, then the error is simply corrected.

What kinds of decisions are fiduciary decisions?

First, we can exclude things that are not fiduciary duties. These include preparing reports to the government and employees, overseeing plan administration, and calculating and explaining benefits, processing claims, and other record-keeping tasks.

Specific fiduciary duties include the following:

1. Buying and selling plan assets, including employer stock.
2. Hiring qualified advisors.
3. Determining that the ESOP is paying no more than fair market value for any stock it acquires.
4. Assuring that the plan is operated in accordance with plan documents and ERISA; if the two conflict, ERISA rules govern.
5. Making sure the terms of any ESOP loans are reasonable.
6. Voting or directing the tendering of shares in the trust for which plan and ERISA rules do not require pass-through voting.
7. Deciding whether to follow participant voting or tendering directions on unallocated or undirected shares.
8. Responding to legitimate offers to purchase the company.
9. Acting to protect plan interests with respect to corporate actions that could harm the interests of plan participants. See the following question for more detail on this issue.

No. 4, of course, is very broad. It can include a variety of decisions. For instance, a fiduciary could be sued for failing to allow employees to vote their shares on required issues, for not giving employees appropriate information to make decisions when they vote, for failing to distribute benefits according to plan rules, for acting in a discriminatory manner in honoring put options, or for failing to assure the filing of reports so that the plan loses its qualified status.

What happens if a fiduciary violates its obligations?

The fiduciary can be sued and is personally responsible for any losses caused by the breach of its duties.

Can the fiduciary be indemnified or insured?

Companies can indemnify the fiduciary by promising to pay the costs of any judgments, but doing so could persuade a court that the ESOP itself is ultimately the fiduciary if the money effectively would reduce the value of employee accounts. Fiduciaries should obtain fiduciary liability insurance, which the company may pay for.

Can employees or the ESOP prevent an undesired acquisition?

ESOP fiduciaries face a dilemma when someone makes an offer to buy ESOP shares for much more than their current price. Can the trustee say no? If the trustee must maximize shareholder value for participants, shouldn't a higher offer be automatically accepted?

The answer is "not necessarily." First, the trustee is allowed to argue that the proposal will improve share value only in the short run; the trustee can look to the long run on this matter. Second, the company can write in its plan document that maintaining employee ownership is one of the plan's objectives. If the acquiring company does not want to continue employee ownership, this could help the fiduciary reject a bid, although that factor alone is not enough on which to base the decision (it can only be one of several considerations). Third, the company can pass through the decision on the matter to participants, subject to the constraints outlined in the employee voting section. This, in itself, may deter potential acquirers. None of these approaches will "bullet-proof" a company, but it should be sufficient to prevent all but the most exceptional bids. Indeed, we do not know of any private companies with ESOPs that have been forced into acquisitions, and of only a few public companies that have.

ESOP Administrative Committees

What is an ESOP administrative committee?

A committee, usually appointed by the board of directors, oversees day-to-day operations of the plan. It is often called the ESOP administrative committee or plan administration committee. In what follows, the term "ESOP administrative committee" is used for all of these committees.

Does every ESOP company have to have an ESOP administrative committee?

No. All ESOPs must have a trustee and someone to administer the plan, but there is no legal requirement that there be an ESOP administrative committee. In practice, however, plan documents almost always specify that there be such a committee or a board of ESOP trustees to administer the plan and oversee its operations.

Is the ESOP administrative committee the same as the plan fiduciary or the plan trustee?

A plan fiduciary is the person or body that makes decisions affecting the plan. ESOPs have named fiduciaries, which can be anyone or any group (the board, the trustee, management, the ESOP administrative committee, all individual plan participants, or anyone else). Just because the plan names a fiduciary, however, does not mean that someone else cannot act as a fiduciary by making a decision about the operation of the plan. An ESOP administrative committee can both be named as a fiduciary and act as a fiduciary even if it is not so named. It can also serve as the plan trustee. The ESOP administrative committee, however, can play neither role if it does not make decisions, but simply renders advice to the fiduciary or trustee.

What do the ESOP administrative committees typically do?

They may be responsible for plan design, including recommending amendments to the plan to the board. In some cases, this could involve fiduciary issues, such as changing the plan in a way that reduces promised benefits to participants beyond the specific ESOP exceptions to

ERISA. They can also make fiduciary decisions for the plan directly or by directing the plan's trustee to make the decision. Alternatively, they can just be advisors to the fiduciaries. They often assume responsibility for administrative oversight of the plan (making sure that statements go out, that participants are paid, that allocations are properly made, etc.), although they rarely actually do the administration. Finally, they often communicate the plan to participants and even oversee the company's employee involvement program. Each of these areas is discussed separately below.

What would be examples of fiduciary decisions an ESOP administrative committee might make?

Fiduciary decisions include, but are not be limited to, determining the voting of shares in the ESOP where the law does not require a pass-through of voting rights to participants, deciding how to invest plan assets both in employer stock and other investments, selling stock, assuring that the ESOP pays no more than fair market value, selecting qualified advisors, assuring that the operation and design of the plan comply with ERISA, and moving assets from the ESOP to another plan. The committee may implement these decisions itself or direct the trustee to carry them out.

In contrast, recommending to the board of directors that the plan be changed or even terminated, voting for board members, and administering the plan in compliance with the law are not normally fiduciary acts.

What are the ESOP administrative committee's legal constraints in deciding how to vote or direct the selling of ESOP shares?

Legally, the ESOP administrative committee must make any decision as to the voting or tendering of shares (other than those for which the plan provides a pass-through to participants) based on the best interests of plan participants as participants. In other words, the ESOP committee (or any other fiduciary) cannot consider the employment interests of participants. Instead, the committee must look to the long-term value of the accounts in the plan. Many consultants would argue that the committee may also consider the preservation of employee ownership as part of the legitimate interests of participants, provided this is spelled out in the plan document. The committee cannot make a decision that is primarily for the benefit of other parties, such as managers or other owners.

Even where the employees direct the voting or tendering of shares, however, there is disagreement on whether the ESOP administrative committee (or other fiduciary) can simply follow these instructions, and, if so, when. This issue is discussed in detail in the section in this chapter on voting.

What are typical administrative oversight responsibilities of the ESOP administrative committee?

The list is long, but here are some of the key issues:

1. Keeping minutes of committee meetings.
2. Making sure the plan administrator gets everyone who is qualified into the plan, and that once they are there, they get their proper allocations and statements, and that the administrator gets notice of forfeitures.
3. Making sure the administrator files the proper reports with the government, obtains the necessary forms for spousal consent, follows the plan's procedures for re-including people who have left the company and returned, etc.
4. Guaranteeing that proper procedures are followed when employees complain about the plan and that other employee rights, such as voting and the opportunity to inspect plan documents, are provided.
5. Hiring a plan administrator and an investment manager for non-stock assets in the plan.
6. Assuring that contributions to the plan are properly credited.
7. Overseeing plan distributions to assure they are done properly.
8. Having a repurchase obligation study conducted and creating a plan to deal with the issues it raises (this may also be a responsibility of the company, however).
9. Interpreting plan provisions.

10. Adopting any additional plan operation rules that may be necessary to make specific what may have been general plan provisions (e.g., plans sometimes provide discretion to their ESOP administrative committees about when to make certain distributions, provided they are made in a nondiscriminatory way and are spelled out in written policy).
11. Providing the administrator with the information needed to operate the plan, and getting from the administrator the information the company needs to file tax reports.

This may sound like a daunting list, but in practice the plan's administrator does most of the work. The ESOP administrative committee must make sure that administrator is competent and must oversee its functioning, however.

How are ESOP administrative committee members chosen?

Because many of the committee's functions are inherently the board's duties, most ESOP administrative committees are board-appointed. Other than general legal and fiduciary concerns, however, no rules govern who can be on the ESOP administrative committee or how they should be selected. In many companies, the committee consists of managers and/or board members; in some, a single manager is the whole committee. More participative companies get nonmanagement employees involved as minority or majority committee members. Usually, other employees elect these, but sometimes management appoints them or they are simply volunteers.

What other kinds of ESOP committees are there besides the ESOP administrative committee?

Many companies have something they call an "ESOP advisory committee," which has no administrative or fiduciary functions. Instead, these committees typically deal with ownership culture issues, such as communicating the plan to other employees, designing and overseeing employee involvement and education programs, and organizing celebrations and events.

How are members of ESOP committees that do not deal with administrative or fiduciary matters selected?

Companies can do this any way they choose. In most cases, however, committee members are elected by their peers or simply volunteer. (There may not be enough people wanting to run to make elections worthwhile.) In some cases, the board selects committee members.

CHAPTER TWO

ESOP Participants and Shareholder Rights

James Steiker

Employee stock ownership plans (ESOPs) are about ownership. Corporate stock ownership through an ESOP is a "mediated" relationship. ESOP participants are intended beneficiaries rather than direct owners. While many companies establish ESOPs to allow participants to feel and act like owners, the ESOP's legal stock share ownership rests with one or more trustees who exercise the rights of ownership, subject to exceptions set forth in the law or in the implementing documents. This chapter describes ESOP participant entitlement to the rights and benefits of corporate stock ownership.

ESOP participant rights are governed primarily by the Employee Retirement Income Security Act of 1974 (ERISA). Corporate shareholder rights are granted under the corporate law of the state of incorporation. This chapter uses Pennsylvania corporate law where state corporate laws apply.

Rights of Stock Ownership

In the United States, most businesses of significant size and scope are owned and operated through corporations. Corporations are legal "persons" that have all of the general powers and legal capacity of a "natural person."[1]

---

1. Pennsylvania Business Corporation Law of 1988, 15 Pa.C.S. §§ 1501-1502 (hereinafter referred to as "PBCL").

Corporations issue shares that represent a portion of ownership. The shares are personal property of the shareholder and represent entitlement to a proportional ownership of the corporation, and voting, dividend, conversion, redemption, liquidation, and other rights.[2]

Under Pennsylvania corporate law, shareholders have certain enumerated rights relating to corporate governance, corporate information, and tendering shares. Corporate governance rights consist generally of the right to get notice of shareholder meetings and the right to one vote per share owned in the election or removal of directors of the corporation, in proposed "fundamental changes" to the corporation, and in certain other corporate decisions.

A corporation must hold at least one meeting of shareholders annually.[3] Each shareholder is entitled to five days' notice of any shareholder meeting (ten days for "fundamental changes").[4] Any notice of a special meeting must specify the general nature of the business to be transacted.[5] Shareholders entitled to cast at least 20% of the votes that all shareholders are entitled to cast may call a special meeting of shareholders at any time as long as they give proper notice.[6] Special meetings of the shareholders may also be called at any time by the board of directors or by such officers or other persons as may be provided in the bylaws.[7]

The bylaws of the corporation operate as regulations for its shareholders, for instance, setting forth the specific time for the annual meeting and general procedures for shareholder meetings. The statute provides certain general rights, including the right of each shareholder to inspect a complete list arranged in alphabetical order of those entitled to vote at any meeting of shareholders[8] and the right to designate a proxy to vote on his or her behalf.[9]

---

2. See, e.g., PBCL § 1521.
3. PBCL § 1755.
4. PBCL § 1704.
5. Id.
6. PBCL § 1755(b)(2).
7. PBCL § 1755(b).
8. PBCL § 1764(a).
9. PBCL § 1759.

Shareholders may elect or remove directors by vote of a majority of shares.[10] They may also vote to adopt, amend, or repeal the bylaws.[11] Shareholders must also approve any "fundamental changes" to the corporation, including amendment of the articles of incorporation, merger or consolidation, share exchanges, disposition of substantially all assets, division, conversion to nonprofit status, or voluntary dissolution.[12]

Corporations must provide each shareholder with an annual financial statement, including at least a balance sheet and a statement of income and expenses. The statements must be mailed within 120 days of the close of the corporation's fiscal year and must include a report by the accountant, if the accountant prepares the statements, or a statement by the person in charge of the corporation's financial records.[13] In lieu of mailing the statements, the corporation may send them by facsimile, e-mail, or other electronic transmission.[14]

Shareholders in privately held companies who properly dissent from certain corporate actions may demand payment from the corporation for the fair value of their shares.[15] Corporate actions subject to dissent include special treatment of shareholders of the same class, mergers, consolidations, share exchanges, divisions, conversions, and certain asset transfers.[16]

ESOPs as Shareholders

ESOPs are employee benefit plans and are primarily regulated under ERISA and related sections of the Internal Revenue Code of 1986, as amended (the "Code"). An ESOP is designed to invest primarily in stock of the employer that sponsors it.[17] The trustee is required to have ex-

---

10. PBCL §§ 1725, 1726.
11. PBCL § 1504.
12. PBCL, Chapter 19.
13. PBCL § 1554.
14. PBCL § 1554(a).
15. PBCL § 1574.
16. PBCL § 1571.
17. Treas. Reg. 54.4975-11(b). ("A plan constitutes an ESOP only if the plan specifically states that it is designed to invest primarily in qualifying securities.")

clusive authority for managing and controlling plan assets unless plan documents delegate that authority to a "named fiduciary."[18]

ESOPs may acquire stock of the sponsor only if such stock constitutes "employer securities" as defined in the Code. Employer securities are readily tradable common stock, or, if a corporation does not have that, then the securities are common stock that has voting power and dividend rights equal to those of the class of common stock with the greatest such rights.[19] An ESOP may acquire non-callable preferred stock so long as it is convertible at any time to common stock that meets the definition of employer securities and the conversion price is reasonable.[20]

ESOP Special Voting Rights

ESOPs must grant special voting rights to participants with respect to employer securities held by the plan. Participants are permitted to instruct the trustee as to all voting of shares of company stock allocated to the participant's account if the employer-sponsor has a registration-type class of securities (e.g., a class of publicly traded securities).[21] ESOPs in privately held companies must permit each participant to instruct the trustee on how to vote the shares allocated to his or her account when a proposal would merge, consolidate, recapitalize, reclassify, liquidate, dissolve, or sell substantially all assets of the company.[22] An ESOP may grant participants broader voting rights than provided by the Code. For instance, an ESOP may grant to participants the right to vote for the board of directors of the company. These additional rights could be granted just on vested shares, although that is not common practice.

Voting of Unallocated Shares

The trustee of the ESOP generally retains the power to vote on behalf of shares held by the ESOP but not yet allocated to participant accounts.

---

18. ERISA § 403(a).
19. Code § 409(l).
20. Code § 409(l)(3).
21. Code § 409(e)(1).
22. Code § 409(e)(2).

Although the issue has been raised primarily in connection with tender offers for ESOP shares, both the courts and the Department of Labor (DOL) have shown hostility toward participant direction of unallocated securities. One court flatly concluded that it would be a breach of the trustee's fiduciary duty to permit participant direction concerning tender of unallocated shares.[23] The DOL has asserted that participants may be considered "named fiduciaries" only for the limited purpose of giving directions to a trustee with regard to tender of stock in their individual accounts. The DOL's position is that tender of unallocated shares is "the exclusive responsibility of the trustee" regardless of plan provisions, and that the decision to tender implies the trustee's general fiduciary duty to determine the prudence of tender.[24]

Directed Voting of Allocated Shares

The courts and regulators have looked more kindly upon participant directions concerning shares allocated to participant accounts. In addition to clear statutory approval for this form of direction (see, e.g., Code Section 409(e)), the DOL has indicated comfort with ESOP participants directing the trustee in certain ESOP decisions.[25] But it has focused on procedural requirements to insure that directions are "proper" and on trustees' ultimate responsibility to take a directed action only if it is consistent with ERISA.[26] In the DOL's view, directions are proper when the participants make independent, uncoerced, and fully informed decisions in the absence of false and misleading information.[27] The DOL's focus on procedural fairness leads it to conclude, however, that

---

23. *Danaher Corp. v. Chicago Pneumatic Tool Co.*, 633 F. Supp. 1066 (S.D.N.Y. 1986).
24. DOL Op. Ltr. re: *Polaroid Stock Equity Plan*, 1989 Lexis 51; 16 BNA Pension Reporter 390 (Feb. 23, 1989).
25. Id.
26. DOL Op. Ltr. re: *Profit-Sharing Retirement Income Plan for the Employees of Carter Hawley Hale Stores, Inc.*, 1984 WL 469057 (Apr. 30, 1984).
27. Id. See also Secretary of Labor's Amicus Brief in *Harris v. Texas Air Corp.*, Civil Nos. 87-2057, 87-2143, 87-2226 and 87-2266 (D.D.C.), summarized in Rizzo et al., "ESOP Case Law: Fiduciary and Corporate Sponsor Concerns," *Journal of Employee Ownership Law and Finance* 4, no. 2 (spring 1992).

if "participant employees are subject to pressure from the employer to vote their shares in a particular manner, it would be the duty of the trustee to ignore any direction given that is the result of such pressure."[28] In the absence of affirmative directions regarding allocated shares, the trustee must take exclusive responsibility for decisions regarding those shares.[29] An ESOP may permit participants to direct the trustee concerning plan investments and tendering of shares, including buying and selling employer stock, but participants are not automatically entitled to give such direction, except when participants who are 55 years or older diversify their accounts.[30]

Participant direction concerning purchase and sale of employer stock in a privately held company may raise issues concerning compliance with federal and state securities laws.[31] Some companies have dealt with this by having employees vote in a non-binding advisory election.

The trustee does not have an unbridled obligation to follow proper participant directions concerning the voting and tender of employer securities. ERISA requires that a trustee act in accordance with the ESOP document only to the extent that it is consistent with the trustee's other fiduciary duties as set forth in ERISA.[32] The trustee must therefore determine whether participant directions are for the exclusive purposes of providing benefits and defraying reasonable expenses and if they are prudent.[33]

There may be a greater practical hurdle to trustee override of participant directions concerning voting of employer securities (as opposed to tender of employer securities). The decision to tender can be quanti-

---

28. DOL Op. Ltr. Apr. 30, 1984.
29. *Reich v. Nationsbank of Ga., N.A.*, 1995 U.S. Dist. WL 316550, 19 Employee Benefits Cas. (BNA) 1345 (N.D. Ga. Mar. 29, 1995).
30. Code § 401(a)(28)(A) (ESOP participants 55 or older with more than 10 years of participation under the ESOP may direct the plan as to investment of 25% of his or her account; this percentage increases to 50% for participants 60 years or older with 16 or more years of participation under the plan).
31. *International Bhd. of Teamsters v. Daniel*, 439 U.S. 551, 99 S. Ct. 790, 58 L. Ed. 2d 808 (1979) (employee interests in employee benefit plans are not securities absent voluntary contributions or voluntary participation).
32. ERISA § 404(a)(1)(D).
33. ERISA § 404(a).

fied to a significant degree and involves a direct financial judgment. A trustee can expect scrutiny of the decision to tender based upon financial results to participants.

The decision to vote employer securities for or against certain directors, in contrast, is likely not quantifiable. Unless the candidate favored by participants is clearly inappropriate or lacks qualifications, it is extremely difficult for a trustee to determine compulsion to override their directions.

Pass-Through of Incidental Ownership Rights

ERISA is silent as to pass-through of other incidental rights of stock ownership to plan participants. While the ESOP trustee may act as shareholder on behalf of the plan to exercise the rights granted to shareholders under corporate law, including obtaining corporate information and examining corporate records, the trustee has no direct duty to convey this information to plan participants. The trustee also has no direct duty to convey information received in its capacity as trustee, such as the appraisal report regarding the value of company stock prepared by an independent appraiser. Participants have only the right to the reporting and disclosure set forth in Title I of ERISA regarding plan investments and individual benefits and options under the plan. Participants may obtain additional information held by the trustee "only to the extent that they relate to the provision of benefits or the defrayment of (plan) expenses."[34]

There may be some linkage, however, between the trustee's fiduciary duty, ability to obtain relevant corporate information, and obligation to honor plan participants' voting instructions on pass-through matters specified in Code Section 409(e) or on additional pass-through voting or tender matters set forth in plan documents. For instance, assume that a privately held 51% ESOP-owned corporation receives a merger offer from a publicly held corporation. The merger offer, by its terms, would render the ESOP a minority rather than a majority shareholder.

---

34. *Acosta v. Pacific Enterprises*, 950 F.2d 611, 14 Employee Benefits Cas. (BNA) 1981 (9th Cir. 1991).

At the same time, the merger offer, set forth as an exchange of the ESOP sponsor's stock for that of the company making the offer, appears, based upon current public market prices, to provide the ESOP with public company shares having a value significantly in excess of the current appraised value of the privately held company shares held by the ESOP (either on its face or in the opinion of a financial advisor).

The plan document must provide that participants direct the trustee as to voting of ESOP shares for or against the merger. Participants would undoubtedly deem relevant both current financial information regarding the prospects of the ESOP company and the most recent independent appraisal of ESOP stock. The trustee's fiduciary duty (and vulnerability to third-party legal action) probably dramatically increases if plan participants do not have access to all available information when they tell the trustee how to vote on the merger. This is certainly the position of the DOL.[35]

Could a plan participant successfully sue for information in the above hypothetical situation? A fiduciary must act prudently on behalf of plan participants and for the exclusive purpose of providing benefits and defraying reasonable expenses. How might a fiduciary demonstrate that it is prudent to withhold information from plan participants as they decide whether to exchange all of the assets held by the plan for essentially a different investment? The answer appears to be that it cannot.

This analysis probably does not extend, however, to incidental rights of ownership unrelated to ESOP participants' exercise of voting rights. For instance, it is hard to argue that, absent specific plan provisions, a trustee should pass through to ESOP participants the right to call a special meeting of shareholders. Indeed, it would be quite difficult for ESOP participants to prove, absent highly unusual circumstances, that a trustee's calling of or failure to call a special meeting of shareholders, by itself, constitutes a breach of fiduciary duty.

Similarly, the dissenter's rights granted by statute to Pennsylvania corporation shareholders probably do not apply to ESOP participants, absent specific plan provisions, even if an ESOP participant instructs the trustee to reject a proposed "fundamental change" to the corporation. For instance, imagine in the earlier hypothetical that an ESOP participant voted against the merger and instructed the trustee to exercise dissenter's

---

35. DOL Op. Ltr Apr. 30, 1984; *Harris v. Texas Air Corp.*

rights. That is ultimately a decision to sell the dissenter's shares, which is an investment decision. If, as in most cases, the decision to tender stock is reserved to the trustee, then the ability to exercise dissenter's rights as a mechanism to force redemption of shares is probably also exclusively a decision of the trustee. The trustee, of course, must as part of its fiduciary duty consider whether to exercise dissenter's rights as to some or all of the ESOP's shares, and a disgruntled participant may ultimately litigate whether that duty was properly exercised.

Conclusion

Shareholders have significant rights in a Pennsylvania corporation beyond voting on "fundamental changes" as set forth in Code Section 409(e)(2). The plan fiduciary has the legal duty to exercise these rights on behalf of the ESOP and no direct obligation to pass through these rights to ESOP participants. ESOP participants have no formal right to information about the employer company generally available to corporate shareholders. The trustee may, however, be obligated to provide additional corporate information to ESOP participants to the extent necessary for them to exercise voting rights set forth by statute or in the plan document. The trustee's exercise or failure to exercise incidental shareholder rights also is part of the fiduciary duty and is subject to review in the same manner as a trustee's performance of other fiduciary duties such as voting and tender.

CHAPTER THREE

Shareholder Obligations of the ESOP Trustee

Brian Ippensen
Merri Ash

To understand trustees' duties, one must understand how corporations are structured and who owns them. Corporations are formalized, legal entities. That is, they exist by virtue of governing statutes. They are created for the sole purpose of conducting business. From a legal standpoint, a corporation is an artificial person, and as such can enter into contracts, hire employees, acquire assets, incur liabilities, and be sued. Titles to property are in the name of the corporation, and, generally, liabilities are limited to the assets of the corporation.

Corporations differ from sole proprietorships and partnerships in their ownership makeup. Individuals own sole proprietorships. Partnerships are arrangements by two or more entities, including corporations, that allow those parties to share the common purposes and risks of the enterprise. Sole proprietorships and partnerships can cease to exist when any one individual or entity leaves. These forms of organization are clearly tied to their owners.

Corporations are owned by stockholders, who can be individuals, other corporations, or trusts, to name a few. The transfer of ownership among these stockholders has no effect on the continuity of the corporation. Because it is distinctly separated from individual stockholders, a corporation has a perpetual life. Each individual stockholder has a duty to treat every other shareholder fairly.

The responsibilities of the ESOP shareholder are at least as great as those of other shareholders in the same corporation. Generally, the corporation's charter will outline shareholders' privileges, such as voting rights, dividend receipt rights, rights to inspect corporate books and records, and the right to sue the corporation for wrongful acts (see the chapter "ESOP Participants and Shareholder Rights" for details). These rights vary by state. They are very important in protecting shareholders against poor management. Thus ESOP trustees must understand what rights they have as holders of corporate shares.

Shares of the ESOP must be held in trust. As a shareholder, the ESOP trustee must act in a fair and reasonable manner with respect to other shareholders while also performing the fiduciary duties for the trust and its beneficiaries. A trustee is a fiduciary under the rules of the Employee Retirement Income Security Act of 1974 (ERISA), because it has discretionary authority over the investment of trust assets. All of the ESOP trustee decisions are subject to the fiduciary requirements of ERISA, including the duty to act prudently and carefully, the duty to act only in the interest of the ESOP participants, and the duty of strict loyalty to the ESOP participants.

Roles and Issues for Trustees in Electing the Board

ESOP trustees must play active roles in the election of a corporation's board of directors. The board is responsible for directing the corporation and its senior managers, who conduct the company's day-to-day affairs. Their decisions will largely determine the value of the corporation and ultimately the value of the shareholders' investment.

Ideally, a group from the board, often a nominating committee, will present a slate of directors. The committee should examine each potential nominee's qualifications, including experience, relationship to the corporation, age, and investment in the corporation, whether as a shareholder or through some other arrangement. The ESOP may provide for voting on directors to be passed through to plan participants. If so, the ESOP trustee has a duty to send relevant information to and obtain instructions from the participants. After receipt, the ESOP trustee should summarize the direction results to draw a consensus from the plan participants. The ESOP plan document will generally state how the trustee is to vote. Some plans provide for participant direction; most provide that the trustee either make an independent decision or follow the directions of a third party (often the board itself). In this case, the third party becomes a co-fiduciary to the decision. Ultimately, though, the ESOP trustee must evaluate the slate of potential directors, determine whether their qualifications are acceptable, and vote the trust's shares as he or she believes is in the best interests of the plan participants. While it would be very rare for a trustee whose actions are directed by employees or another entity to override these directions, ERISA does provide that if the trustee believes that not doing so would violate the law or the plan, or is clearly not in the best interests of plan participants, then the trustee should act to protect those interests.

Several issues can develop and must be addressed by the ESOP trustee:

- Board member qualifications: In order to vote for a candidate, the trustee must believe that candidate possesses the qualities necessary to effectively direct the corporation and its management. If the candidate was nominated by the board, the trustee must also have faith in the board's effectiveness before agreeing with its choice.

- Participant direction contrary to board nomination: When participants are given the opportunity to direct their shares, they may not agree with board nominations. Personality issues may arise, particularly if the board nominee is also an employee supervisor. For example certain decisions made by a supervisor may be unpopular among the ESOP participants but be necessary for the business. Or a number of participants may write in an alternative candidate. Personality issues can influence a participant's vote. The ESOP trustee needs to understand these issues but must also determine the best candidate for the corporation's board. Again, this situation is extremely rare—participants tend to be conservative voters—but requires trustee attention.

- Exertion of undue influence over participants as to how they should vote: Participants must be able to direct their votes without undue influence from members of the board, management, or other employees. Participants should be encouraged to express their views by voting but cannot be coerced into particular yes or no votes.

- Voting direction confidentiality: Participants must have confidence that their votes are recorded discretely. A participant who votes against the recommendations of management or the board should not have to worry about who will discover their particular voting selection. Without confidence in the voting process, participants may be reluctant to participate.

- Multiple sets of board nominations: While this is unlikely to be an issue in privately held companies, interested parties can present additional slates of directors. The other party may be a dissenting shareholder who believes the current board is not meeting appropriate performance standards or has made poor decisions. If participant direction is sought, the ESOP trustee must give equal consideration to both slates of directors. The ESOP trustee now must decide among the alternatives available with the aid of the participants' direction. Obviously, the trustee will consider issues of qualification and the implications of voting contrary to the board's recommendation before voting in the best interests of the plan participants.

- Appropriate board composition and structure: The Department of Labor has stated that trustees have an affirmative duty to exercise their shareholder rights to try to assure that the governance of the company is appropriate and effective. This could mean, for instance, voting for directors who favor establishing independent review of executive compensation.

Roles/Issues for Trustees in Responding to Acquisition Proposals

Like any other asset, tangible or otherwise, a corporation has value. Like beauty, the value can be in the eye of the beholder. For example, businesses developing Internet-based products in the 1980s probably had little value in this new frontier. Then, in the mid-1990s, their business values began to increase, and soon people were paying speculatively high amounts. By 2001, many companies had become insolvent, and those remaining had limited value. In a very short span, the industry went through a complete lifecycle.

As companies were merged, acquired, or closed, boards of directors entertained and reviewed many proposals, some with merit, others without. The board has a duty to the shareholders to investigate the merits of each proposal. It cannot simply decide the corporation is not for sale. If the board fails to respond to an offer, it is not fulfilling its duties and could be sued for wrongful acts.

Once the board has determined that an offer to buy the company is legitimate, it must notify its shareholders, including the ESOP trustee. The trustee then must provide sufficient information and request voting instructions from each plan participant, if the transaction is structured so that there is a vote (it could be done as a sale of stock). The information provided to participants to solicit their votes would include the name of the acquiring company, the offer price, and prospective financial statements. If the sale is structured so that a vote is not required, the trustee or ESOP committee could make the decision as to the ESOP shares, unless the plan provides that the participants have the right to direct the trustee as to the tendering of the shares.

The idea of selling the corporation can be emotional for plan participants, especially if layoffs seem likely. Participants directing their votes may not look favorably upon such an offer. The ESOP trustee should seek the advice of legal and financial experts to review the offer. If it is determined to be in the best interests of all plan participants, then the ESOP trustee must consider accepting it.

Several considerations affect how the ESOP trustee acts on unsolicited offers. First, as described in the chapter by James Steiker in this book, the Department of Labor and the courts have generally concurred that when employees direct the trustee as to how to vote their shares in an acquisition proposal, the trustee should go along with those directions absent a compelling reason to believe that the employees are acting contrary to their best interests as plan participants (as opposed to as employees). On unallocated shares, trustees generally must follow their own judgment unless the plan designates employees as named fiduciaries for those shares. Even in this case, however, the trustee has an affirmative obligation to exercise independent judgment in voting these shares, even if contrary to employee directions.

This same theory applies to acquisitions structured as tender offers. Employees do not have an automatic right to direct the tendering of shares in an ESOP (whether in a public or private company). Some plans pass through this right to plan participants, but it is subject to the same fiduciary constraints as voting on an acquisition.

In many cases, an ESOP company will not want to be acquired, even in the face of an attractive offer. The dilemma is that trustees must act to maximize the value of plan assets, which seems to suggest the only answer to a good offer is "yes." Trustees, however, can respond "no," even if the offer is for more than the fair market value, for a number of reasons:

- The courts and the Department of Labor have said that trustees must look to the long-term value of the plan assets; it may be the offer provides a short-term bump, but that the corporation's long-term prospects are better. This may especially be the case if the offer involves exchanging the ESOP stock into stock of the acquirer.
- The trustee must look at the future retirement benefits to participants as a whole. It may be that the ESOP, for instance, still has shares to be allocated, or that future contributions are planned at a high percentage of pay. There may also be other retirement plans operating alongside the ESOP. The acquiring company may offer smaller retirement contributions. So even though the stock price is attractive, employees would receive fewer benefits long term.
- Some plans state that the ESOP's principal purpose is to maintain long-term employee ownership. This may be the weakest legal justification for saying no, but it is still arguably an employee benefit to be considered.

In practice, companies that make it clear that the trustee will consider these issues make themselves relatively unattractive acquisition targets. As a result, unwanted acquisitions are rare. However, in the face of an exceptional offer, an ESOP trustee may still have to say "yes."

More common are solicited offers. Here, the trustees must act aggressively to protect employee interests, seeking to maximize the acquisition's effects on both the share price and the future retirement benefits of the employees. The trustee should be an active negotiator in the transaction, represented by its own independent counsel.

Oversight of Board/Executive Compensation

The rights and privileges of ownership allow the shareholder to review the records of the corporation. If, by election, shareholders determine who is on the board, then one could surmise that they have the right to review the compensation of those individuals. After all, the board members serve at the pleasure of the shareholders. Additionally, the board hires management. The shareholders should be privy to the board's decisions about hiring those individuals and determining their compensation.

Our capitalist system of rewarding good performance with good pay has worked for decades. The ESOP trustee needs to understand how the corporation's performance relates to the compensation paid to the individuals responsible for decision-making. Excessive compensation begins when the performance is less than expected, and when alternative individuals who could improve performance and be paid less are available but not used. It is not unreasonable for the ESOP trustee to request the corporation complete studies on board/executive compensation. Such analysis can benchmark the corporation with its peers.

Every shareholder understands it takes people to make the organization work. Finding the right people with the right qualifications can be a daunting task. Every corporation faces compensation issues. Underpay, and the right people will move on to greener pastures, which will tarnish the corporation's performance; overpay, and the corporation's financial performance will suffer.

In summary, the roles and responsibilities of directors and shareholders are far-reaching and can provide great rewards. The roles and responsibilities of the ESOP trustee are vast and need special attention and care. The duties of shareholder, director, and trustee can coexist. However, the opinions of each group can diverge. Anyone serving as the ESOP trustee must be ready to put the fiduciary duties required by ERISA before his or her duties as shareholder or director.

CHAPTER FOUR

A Practical Guide for Company Stock Fiduciaries

Kelly Q. Driscoll
Alex W. Kirby

Issues involving company stock investments in retirement plans came to the forefront of everyday news during the Enron scandal. Shortly after Employee Retirement Income Security Act (ERISA) litigation was filed in Enron,[1] a significant number of class-action lawsuits alleging breach of fiduciary duty with respect to plan investments in employer securities followed. These suits initially involved companies that experienced serious problems, often coupled with accusations of impropriety on behalf of corporate officers, such as Rite Aid,[2] Global Crossing,[3] and Tyco International,[4] but subsequent suits included companies whose stock had merely experienced a measurable yet often short-lived drop in price. The ERISA claims in these cases generally focus on breach of fiduciary duty, questioning the prudence of maintaining plan investments in company stock and often raising issues of inside information potentially known to internal fiduciaries that was not disclosed to plan participants.

The named defendants in these cases often include individual plan committee members, the plan sponsor, officers or directors responsible

---

1. *Tittle v. Enron Corp. et al.*, Civ. Act. No. H-01-3913 (S.D. Tex.).
2. *Kolar v. Rite Aid Corp.*, 01-CV-1229 (E.D. Pa.).
3. *McAllister v. Winick*, 02-CV-7461 (S.D.N.Y.).
4. *In re Tyco International Ltd. Securities Derivative and "ERISA" Litigation*, 02-MOL-1335-B (D.N.H.).

for appointing plan fiduciaries, and the trustee. Some of the cases allege that conflicts of interest precluded the plan sponsor or internal fiduciaries from investigating the merits of continued investment in company stock. Most charge that the plan sponsor or its officers, who might also have been members of a plan committee, should have disclosed material, non-public information to plan participants who continued to invest in company stock. The complaints typically allege a fiduciary breach for failure to discontinue new purchases of employer securities and failure to sell or liquidate the stock before further price declines. Many of these cases have survived motions to dismiss, although trustees have had success winning several motions to dismiss or motions for summary judgment such as Worldcom,[5] Cardinal Health,[6] RCN,[7] and Solutia.[8] In granting the trustee's motion for summary judgment in the recent United Airlines[9] case, the court cited the "presumption of prudence" standard articulated in the Moench[10] case, which provides that there is a presumption under ERISA that holding company stock is prudent. In the US Airways[11] case, the plaintiffs alleged that Fidelity Management Trust Company, the plan's trustee, should have challenged the decision to put a company stock choice in the company's 401(k) plan based on public information that US Airways was considering filing for bankruptcy. The court cited the Department of Labor's FAB 2004-03 and ERISA Section 403(a) in granting Fidelity's motion to dismiss. The court referenced modern portfolio theory that a risky investment can contribute to the diversification of a portfolio. The court also noted that the plan participants were informed about the importance of diversification as well as given options to diversify along the spectrum from low to high risk.

---

5. *In re Worldcom, Inc. ERISA Litigation,* 02-Civ.-4816 (DLC).
6. *In re Cardinal Health, Inc. ERISA Litigation,* 424 F.Supp.2d 735 (S.D. Ohio 2006).
7. *In re RCN Litigation,* 2006 U.S. Dist. LEXIS 12929 (D.N.J Mar. 21, 2006).
8. *Dickerson v. Feldman* (Solutia ERISA *Litigation*), 426 F.Supp.2d 130 (S.D.N.Y. Mar. 30, 2006).
9. *Summers v. State St. Bank & Trust Co.,* Nos. 05-4005 and 05-4317, 2006 WL 1751888 (7th Cir. June 28, 2006).
10. *Moench v. Robertson,* 62 F.3d 553, 571 (1995).
11. *DiFelice vs. US Airways,* No. 04-889 (E.D. Va. June 26, 2006).

Other cases have settled. Most of the defendants in the Enron ERISA litigation settled under terms which included $85 million paid by Enron, $1.5 million from Enron board members and Enron's former HR director, and $37.5 million paid by the trustee, Northern Trust.[12] Settlement amounts for ERISA claims in other cases include $79 million in Global Crossing,[13] $51 million in Worldcom,[14] $46.5 million in Household International,[15] and $30.75 million in Dynegy.[16]

Although many company stock cases are still outstanding, the initial flurry of new cases being filed has clearly subsided. Most recently, the ERISA litigation trend continues but has taken on a different shape. The plaintiffs' bar has shifted focus from company stock investments to plan expense disputes involving claims of excessive compensation and unreasonable fees. This newer breed of fiduciary breach lawsuits primarily targets plan sponsors and internal fiduciaries with respect to their understanding, decision-making and disclosure of fee arrangements and amounts paid to plan vendors and service providers. Even though these newer cases are quite distinct from the company stock litigation, it is helpful for plan fiduciaries fulfilling broader roles to understand the fiduciary standards established by ERISA. What is evident from cases past and present is that fiduciary process still remains important. While each situation must be considered individually, the following is intended to serve as a general guide for fiduciaries responsible for company stock investments, and some of the basic tenets can be applied on an even broader basis.

Know the ERISA Basics

Section 404(a)(1) of ERISA provides that a fiduciary must "discharge his duties solely in the interest of participants and beneficiaries . . . for the exclusive purpose of providing benefits to participants and beneficiaries and defraying reasonable expenses of administering the plan . . . with

---

12. *In re Enron Corp. ERISA Litigation*, No. H-01-3913 (S.D. Tex.).
13. *In re Global Crossing Ltd.*, No. 02 Civ. 7453 (S.D.N.Y.).
14. *In re Worldcom, Inc. ERISA*, No. 1:02cv4816 (S.D.N.Y.).
15. *In re Household International, Inc. ERISA Litigation*, No. 02 C 7921 (N.D. Ill.).
16. *In re Dynegy, Inc. ERISA Litig.*, No. H-02-3076 (S.D. Tex).

the care, skill, prudence and diligence under the circumstances then prevailing as a prudent man acting in a like capacity and familiar with such matters would use in the conduct of an enterprise of a like character and with like aims . . . by diversifying the investments of the plan so as to minimize the risk of large losses, unless under the circumstances it is clearly prudent not to do so . . . in accordance with the documents and instruments governing the plan insofar as such documents and instruments are consistent with the provisions of Title I of ERISA." These are easily remembered as:

1. *Duty of loyalty:* Act solely in the interest of participants.
2. *Exclusive benefit:* Act only to provide retirement benefits and pay plan expenses.
3. *Prudent expert:* Use due diligence and appropriate expertise.
4. *Diversification:* ERISA offers an exemption for ESOPs and company stock funds in other defined contribution plans to the extent they hold "qualifying employer securities," and offers an exemption from the prudence requirement to the extent that it also requires diversification. However, ESOP fiduciaries still must act prudently concerning whether to buy or sell company stock when they know or should know that the stock is not an appropriate investment.
5. *Pursuant to plan documents:* Follow plan documents to the extent they are consistent with ERISA.

Read the Documents

To understand who the fiduciaries are and what their respective duties are, it is important to read the plan documents and trust agreement. On more than one occasion, plan committee members have thought the company had full responsibility for company stock investments, yet the documents indicated it was the committee's responsibility; or trustees thought they were supposed to be directed (i.e., told what decisions to make by another body or individual and thus partly exempt from fiduciary obligations), but the trust agreement provided them with investment discretion as well as valuation responsibilities; or plan sponsors thought the trustee was the primary fiduciary for company stock, when in fact the trust document looked more like a mere custody agreement. In some documents, the company, acting through its board of directors, is responsible for the company stock investment or for appointing the members of a fiduciary committee for a plan.

Often the committee has the primary responsibility for company stock oversight and for directing the trustee with respect to investments in employer securities. Many institutional trust agreements attempt to limit the trustee's responsibilities to custody-type functions, while others provide the trustee with significant discretion over investments, including company stock. Look in the documents for clear delegation of responsibilities and any limitations on specific duties as well as indemnification provisions. Identify which fiduciary is responsible for determining if the company stock continues to be an appropriate plan investment. The documents are not always clear. Determine whether the plan requires an "exclusive" investment in company stock or provides the fiduciary with greater discretion by requiring only that the plan be "primarily" invested in company stock. Some plans have investment policies or guidelines specific to the company stock investment. Review the voting and tender provisions to see who has primary and residual fiduciary responsibility in exercising these rights.

Also review the summary plan description and other employee communications. If voting or tender rights are passed through to participants, a clear description of those rights and an explanation of how to exercise them should be provided to participants during the voting/tender process.

Appoint and Monitor Competent Plan Fiduciaries

Often the company sponsoring the plan, acting through its board of directors, is responsible for appointing plan fiduciaries such as a plan committee and a trustee. The Department of Labor's long-held position is that the appointment itself is a fiduciary act and carries with it a duty to monitor the performance of the appointed fiduciary.[17] While there is no requirement for a fiduciary to have pre-existing expertise in ERISA or financial matters through course study or seminars, the appointed

---

17. 29 C.F.R. Section 2509.75-8.

fiduciaries should be capable of understanding the responsibilities imposed upon them by ERISA. Individual fiduciaries should also have the ability and adequate resources to hire experts necessary to assist them in acting prudently in the execution of their fiduciary responsibilities. When appointing individuals, review their experience to determine whether they have demonstrated sufficient accomplishments and competent decision-making during their careers. In certain situations, it may be better to exclude individuals who are likely to acquire inside information that might someday present significant conflicts with the fulfillment of plan fiduciary responsibilities. Once appointed, individuals should attend meetings, implement sufficient processes, review investment performance, address appropriate issues, and report back to the board or individuals responsible for monitoring the fiduciaries.

Before appointing an institutional fiduciary or trustee, prepare a list of questions or a written request for proposals and interview several candidates. Determine whether the candidate institution has experience specific to company stock investments and what background or expertise the individuals who would provide the fiduciary services have. Each candidate should describe its general practices for addressing company stock issues. If the trustee is directed with respect to company stock investments, how does the trustee determine whether the directions it receives are "proper"?[18] What type of periodic reporting or presentations will the institution provide so that the appointing body may properly monitor the trustee's performance?

Understand the Company Stock Investment

It is important for the fiduciary to have a general understanding of the operation and composition of the plan's company stock investment. The fiduciary should be aware whether the investments in company stock are elective, mandated, or both (for example, 401(k) deferrals can be invested in company stock at the election of the participant, but

---

18. Under ERISA Section 403(a)(1) a trustee must follow "proper" directions of a named fiduciary which are "not contrary" to Title I of ERISA. Although ERISA is over thirty years old, there is very little law on what the phrase "proper" directions actually means.

matching contributions are required to be invested in company stock). Often the investment has minimum holding requirements or other limitations such as restrictions from transferring to other investment options. Many company stock investments operate in a fund-accounting environment with a cash or short-term investment component. Others are invested strictly in shares of the stock. It is helpful to understand how the liquidity needs of the plan are managed and, if the stock is publicly traded common stock or convertible preferred stock, whether it is registered. All of these facts may affect how a fiduciary monitors the stock investment and determines whether it is appropriate to continue to buy, hold or sell stock.

ESOPs and other eligible individual-account plans, such as 401(k) plans, are exempt from the diversification requirements of ERISA and may invest up to 100% of their assets in employer stock.[19] However, a fiduciary is required to follow a plan document only to the extent the document is consistent with ERISA.[20] The critical question remains—under what circumstances is it inconsistent with ERISA to follow a plan provision that calls for investment in company stock?

Courts have found that if the plan provides for an investment in company stock, then there is a presumption that it is an appropriate investment.[21] It is often asserted that this presumption may be overcome and that at some point it may be imprudent to continue to invest in company stock. The line, however, is anything but clear.[22] What is clear in this post-Enron environment, is that it is risky business for a fiduciary not to monitor the performance of a plan's company stock investment.

If a plan meets all the requirements of Section 404(c) of ERISA and the corresponding regulations, then a safe harbor is provided to shield fiduciaries from liability resulting from a participant's investment decisions. This protection is available only if the participants are provided

---

19. ERISA Sections 404(a)(2) and 407(b)(2).
20. ERISA Section 404(a)(1)(D).
21. *Moench v. Robertson*, 62 F.3d 553 (3d Cir. 1995), *cert. denied*, 516 U.S. 1115 (1996) and *Kuper v. Iovenko*, 66 F.3d 1447 (6th Cir. 1995).
22. *In Re McKesson HBOC, Inc. ERISA Litigation*, 2002 U.S. Dist. LEXIS 19473 (N.D. Cal. 2002), *Nelson v. Ipalco Enterprises, Inc.*, 2003 U.S. Dist. LEXIS 2431 (S.D. Ind. 2003), *Steinman v. Hicks*, 252 F.Supp.2d 746 (C.D. Ill. 2003); cf. *Kuper v. Iovenko*, 66 F.3d 1447 (6th Cir. 1995).

with sufficient information to make reasoned decisions. (Many of the recent cases include claims of misleading disclosures and material misrepresentations that were alleged to have been made to participants.) However, even if the company stock fund investment meets the regulatory requirements, the general fiduciary provisions of ERISA may still apply to the initial designation of the investment alternatives and the ongoing determination that such alternatives remain suitable and prudent options for the plan.[23]

Be Familiar with the Prohibited Transaction Rules

Transactions between a plan and a party-in-interest are generally prohibited under ERISA unless there is an applicable exemption.[24] Acquisitions and sales of "qualifying employer securities" for "adequate consideration" and where no commission is charged to the plan are exempted. Certain ESOP loans are exempted under Section 408(b)(3) of ERISA.

If a class exemption does not exist, a plan can apply for an individual exemption. There are rules prohibiting self-dealing under Section 406(b) of ERISA. The prohibited transaction rules are extensive and relatively complicated. A fiduciary should seek the advice of a qualified legal expert when a company stock transaction involves a party-in-interest.

Establish a Process

In evaluating whether a fiduciary acted in a prudent manner and solely in the interests of the participants, courts and regulators often place as much or more importance on the manner in which a fiduciary arrived at a particular determination as on the actual merits of the decision. To show that a fiduciary exercised procedural prudence in connection with a company stock investment, it is helpful for the fiduciary to have a process for periodically reviewing the company stock investment and performing sufficient due diligence to address issues as they arise.

---

23. See "Final Regulations Regarding Participant Directed Individual Account Plans (ERISA Section 404(c) Plans)," 57 Fed. Reg. 46906, 46922 (Oct. 13, 1992).
24. ERISA Section 406.

A periodic performance review for company stock could be implemented in a manner consistent with the review process for all other retirement plan investments. If the stock is publicly traded, the fiduciary should be aware of dramatic price fluctuations or significant news. If it is stock of a private company, the fiduciary might review, with its valuation advisor, the company's financial reports and any material contingent liabilities. The fiduciary might implement a more active monitoring process or further meet to discuss the company stock investment in certain situations that could include:

- Significant price declines vs. the market or industry peers
- Debt/credit quality deterioration
- Material negative news, such as financial restatements, unexpected earnings results, integrity of executives being questioned, contingent liabilities, or unfavorable court decisions
- Declining volume/float
- Analysts dropping coverage
- Distressed industry
- Potential bankruptcy concerns

The decision to override a plan document, another fiduciary's direction, or a participant's direction to invest in company stock is very serious and generally takes place only in extraordinary situations. However, having an adequate review process that indicates the fiduciary is monitoring the investment and addressing issues when extreme situations occur is a good idea.

Make Reasoned Decisions

A fiduciary must demonstrate substantive prudence by making sound decisions. A thorough evaluation of the merits of the fiduciary's potential actions should be completed before he or she makes a final determination. If the investment becomes a problem, the prudence of continued investment becomes highly suspect, the viability of the company becomes questionable, or the stock experiences a potentially irreversible decline in value, then the fiduciary might consider the following actions:

- Reduce or eliminate transfer restrictions.
- Recommend modifying plan provisions with respect to in-kind matching obligations (plan design change would be a corporate decision).
- Increase the cash position of the company stock fund.
- Suspend or discontinue new investments in the stock.
- Sunset the company stock as an investment option.
- Evaluate an exit or sales strategy.
- Select a default investment.
- Commence a selling program or an orderly liquidation.

Discussing these matters with the plan sponsor may be desirable or essential.

In these problem situations, it is sometimes critical for the fiduciary to have independent expert advice. Retaining independent legal counsel may be desirable, and hiring a financial or investment expert may also be advisable. The retention of an independent fiduciary may be appropriate to avoid potential conflicts of interest.

Donovan v. Bierwirth[25] involved internal plan fiduciaries who were corporate officers actively opposing a takeover attempt. These fiduciaries refused to tender the plan's stock and even had the plan buy more than 1 million additional shares. The court stated that the fiduciaries were required to make all of their decisions with "an eye single" to the interests of the plan and its participants. The court concluded that the fiduciaries should have realized that their fiduciary judgment was biased and that by failing to ensure the plan's interests were properly considered and protected, the trustees breached their duty to act "solely in the interest" of the plan.

Review SEC Issues

If the plan sponsor is publicly traded, certain SEC filings may be involved. If the plan permits participant-directed elective deferrals to be invested in company stock, the issuer of the stock must file a registra-

---

25. 680 F.2d 263 (2nd Cir.), *cert. denied,* 459 U.S. 1069 (1982).

tion statement, usually an S-8 form for the plan. If the Form S-8 is not filed, it does not cover a sufficient number of shares, or the company's financial statements are not current, then the plan may have a right to rescind all stock purchased within the previous year. For example, one of the claims in the Rite Aid case alleged a breach of fiduciary duty for failure to exercise the plan's rescission rights.

Are the plan's purchases and sales of company stock directed by the company or by a committee? The plan may be considered an affiliate of the company for SEC Rule 10b-18 or other purposes and so may be subject to blackout and aggregated volume restrictions. Does the plan own 10% or more of the company? If so, plan sales of company stock may be subject to the filing and disclosure requirements of SEC Rule 144 and further restricted by the amount of stock the plan may sell over a certain period. Does the plan own 5% or more of the company? If so, a Form 13(d) or (g) filing may be necessary. It is helpful for the plan fiduciary to consult with experienced legal counsel when addressing plan and fiduciary issues related to securities laws and regulations.

Document Decisions

Meetings to discuss the fiduciary's responsibilities, due diligence or analysis, potential actions, considerations, and determinations should be documented. The resulting minutes may include the date of the meeting and the names individuals who attended the meeting, including any advisors. Sufficient time should be allotted to fully consider appropriate actions and question advisors. It is often helpful to summarize in the minutes the issues discussed as well as critical questions the committee asks the advisors. Written materials or analysis provided at the meeting should generally be retained. Plan documents should be reviewed and amended to appropriately implement the fiduciary's desired actions. In a recent case where fiduciaries were sued for selling ESOP stock, the court specifically referenced amended plan language that provided them with appropriate discretion to sell ESOP stock to diversify the plan's assets.[26]

---

26. *Thompson v. Avondale Industries Inc.*, 2003 U.S. Dist. LEXIS 2318 (La. 2003).

Litigation/Settlement Decisions

If a plan or its participants has potential claims or if litigation has been initiated, a fiduciary may have to evaluate the potential claims; this sometimes might be hard for an internal fiduciary, because of potential conflict issues. Such claims might include breach of fiduciary duty, prohibited transaction issues, securities law claims, and claims against professionals. The fiduciary should determine whether it is appropriate to pursue the claims, monitor existing litigation, or participate in a class action. In these situations, issues to address may include the sources and appropriateness of the lawsuit; the value of the consideration for potential settlement; the extent of any releases; the basis of the plan's participation in a class action (the trust's trading activity may differ from the participants' trades); and the compensation of legal counsel. The DOL has issued a prohibited transaction class exemption covering situations in which a plan, or fiduciary on behalf of a plan, is considering resolving claims against parties-in-interest in exchange for consideration.[27] The exemption provides guidelines for the fiduciary to follow in such situations.

Conclusion

It is important to remember that fiduciaries do not have to guarantee the results of their decisions and are not expected to accurately predict investment results or market performance.[28] The mere fact that a company's stock price declines after an ESOP or 401(k) plan acquires it is not, in itself, evidence that fiduciaries acted improperly. What fiduciaries are expected to do is act in a diligent, prudent manner with the interests of participants always at the forefront of their determinations.

---

27. 68 FR 75632 (Dec 31, 2003).

28. *Laborers Nat'l Pension Fund v. Northern Trust Quantitative Advisors, Inc.*, 173 F.3d 313, 317 (5th Cir.), *cert. denied.* 528 U.S. 967 (1999); *Lanka v. O'Higgins*, 810 F. Supp. 379, 389 (N.D.N.Y. 1992).

Appendix: Enron and Related Litigation
Corey Rosen

The dramatic drop in stock value held in 401(k) plans and, occasionally, ESOPs in the post-dot-com boom era prompted dozens of lawsuits by current and former plan participants who contended that the management of their plans violated ERISA requirements that plan assets be managed in a prudent and fiduciarily sound manner for the exclusive benefit of plan participants. Typically, plan trustees, plan administrative committee members, board members, company officers, and the company itself were sued. As of mid-2007, 53 of these lawsuits had been settled or judgments reached. These judgments and settlements came to $1.47 billion (including attorney fees and court costs) spread over approximately 1.3 million participants. Just four of the cases (Enron, Royal Dutch Shell, the Williams Companies, and AOL/Time Warner) totaled $557 million of the $1.47 billion. Many cases are still in process and could take years to resolve.

All but a few of these lawsuits were in public companies, and fewer than 10 have involved ESOPs. While this is a very different demographic from that of the typical reader of this book (someone at a closely held ESOP company), these cases have presented a number of lessons worth heading as to how the law will affect plans with employer stock. This appendix highlights a few of the key cases. More detailed discussions can be found in the NCEO's annual legal update issue of the *Journal of Employee Ownership Law and Finance*

The Enron Case

The seminal case in this area remains Enron (*Chao v. Enron Corp*). The Department of Labor sued the fiduciaries of Enron's 401(k) plan and ESOP for improperly encouraging employees to invest in Enron stock and for continuing to hold Enron shares in the plan when there were reasons to believe that was not prudent. Enron's 401(k) plan was primarily invested in Enron shares, and the ESOP was essentially entirely invested in the stock. The two plans owned more than 25 million shares in 2001. Charged as fiduciaries were the plans' administrative committees, Enron Corporation, Kenneth Lay, and Jeffrey Skilling (the former CEO and CFO of the company), Enron's board, and the plans themselves. The suit alleged that the administrative committees, despite many signs of problems, never monitored plan holdings of Enron shares, never questioned or slowed investment in these shares, never considered the prudence of concentrating assets in Enron shares, and never considered freezing or removing Enron shares as an investment option for employees. Two of the members of the committee, the DOL alleged, had specific information that accounting and financial irregularities were about to cause serious problems. Enron, although not a named fiduciary, never sought to monitor the committee, remove its members, or correct misstatements by Kenneth Lay regarding Enron's financial condition. Lay and Skilling also never monitored the committee, never supplied it with adverse information they had about the company, and Lay misled participants about the company's financial condition, even encouraging them to buy shares when he knew that problems were coming. The board was accused of having failed to appoint a trustee to manage the ESOP's holding of shares and of never having performed that duty itself. Other lawsuits were filed by participants and later consolidated into a single case (*Tittle v. Enron Corp*).

The Department of Labor argued that a company's board and management have a fiduciary liability for the operation of an ERISA plan as a result of their appointment of (and presumed ability to remove) designated fiduciaries for the plan, even if management or the board does not actually make decisions concerning plan investments. The DOL also argued that plan fiduciaries should take actions to protect participants from over-investing in company stock when they have reason to know the stock price will go down.

Enron and other cases raise a variety of issues, only some of which are directly relevant to corporate governance issues in an ESOP company. For instance, whether the board is responsible for monitoring the plan fiduciaries it appoints is clearly a crucial issue. Other key governance issues concern whether and when fiduciaries should stop buying or should sell company stock in the face of economic difficulties, what kinds of information to disclose to plan participants about the company's financial state, and when board members or officers are considered fiduciaries of the plan. Some other issues these lawsuits raise, such as who has standing in a class action, or how long participants can wait to sue, are legally interesting but not directly relevant here.

Because the Enron case was never fully adjudicated, we will never know how the courts would have responded to these specific concerns. But several other important cases provide some guidance. The courts generally have taken a more restrictive view of the responsibilities of the board, management, and company, often concluding they are not fiduciaries simply by virtue of their appointment powers. Rather, the courts have looked to actions these bodies or individuals may have taken to influence or control fiduciary decisions. Similarly, the courts have tended to favor the assumption that fiduciaries should retain employer stock in a plan unless there is good reason to believe the company is in serious difficulty (and even then, there may be reasons not to sell stock). But these decisions should provide only limited comfort. Just facing a lawsuit is painful enough, even if the plaintiffs lose. But while the courts have generally taken positions relatively favorable to ESOP trustees, plans that lack the kind of protections and practices described in the chapter for which this is an appendix could face severe penalties. The risk is even greater if these plans allow for, or worse, encourage employee investment in company stock.

In *Williams Cos. ERISA Litigation,* No. 02-CV-153-H (N.D. Okla. July 14, 2003), for instance, a district court held that fiduciaries were liable for failing to provide participants with proper information about the plan, but dismissed the board and the company from the lawsuit, saying that their power to appoint and remove fiduciaries was a plan settlor issue, not a fiduciary issue. Courts reached a similar decision on both the information and settlor issues in *Crowley v. Corning, Inc.,* No. 02-CV-6172 CJS (W.D.N.Y. 2002) and in *Stein v. Smith,* No. 01-10500-RCL (D. Mass. July 3, 2003). In both cases, company stock (Corning, Inc., and Stone & Webster) declined sharply, partly due to accounting and earnings projections irregularities.

In *Kling v. Fidelity Management.* No. 01-CV-119939-MEL (D. Mass. June 3, 2003), a court ruled that an employee could sue Fidelity Management Trust as a directed trustee of Harnischferger's 401(k) plan. The company's stock was an optional investment in the 401(k) plan. Accounting irregularities led to the company's bankruptcy. Kling sued Fidelity as well as the company. Fidelity sought to dismiss the suit, saying it was a directed trustee; the court ruled that as such, it could not be sued simply for investing in company stock, but it could be liable if the jury found it followed directions contrary to ERISA. By contrast, in *In re McKesson,* No. COO-020030 RMW (N.D. Cal. 2002), a court ruled that fiduciaries did not have to inform participants of a likely impending drop in McKesson stock, because to do so would have required them to disclose information about an accounting irregularity that they knew would be soon announced. Informing participants would have violated securities laws, the court concluded, and the fiduciaries were not obligated to violate one set of laws to conform to another. A detailed description of these differing views can be found in Glenn Sulzer, "Labor Department and Courts at Odds Over Fiduciary Liability for Declines in Employer Stock," *Employee Benefit Plan Review,* July 2003.

In two other recent cases, courts have taken a narrow view of when employees can sue over stock declines in an ESOP. In *Lalonde v. Textron Inc.,* No. 02-334s (D.R.I. June 24, 2003), a district court ruled that fiduciaries were not responsible for the decline in Textron stock. The company's ESOP allowed employees to invest in the stock, which the company matched with additional shares. Plaintiffs alleged plan fiduciaries, who were Textron executives, encouraged employees to invest, even though the company was going through difficult times. The court ruled that the "special nature" of ESOPs entitles fiduciaries to a presumption that company stock is a reasonable investment. In any event, the court said, Textron's stock fell with the market (from $73 to $41 over two years). The court also rejected arguments against self-dealing and anti-inurement. Finally, it ruled that for the fiduciaries to dump Textron stock would have caused further declines in share price.

In *Stein,* the court refused to dismiss a lawsuit brought by former Stone & Webster employees alleging that the company should have changed its policy of investing in company stock in an ESOP and 401(k) plan, particularly since plan fiduciaries knew that the company stock would be under pressure from underbidding on contracts that led to undisclosed losses. Unlike in *McKesson,* the court ruled that potential conflicts with securities laws do not preclude taking actions to protect plan participants from imprudent investments in company stock. The court said that the decision to invest in company stock is a settlor function but that the decision not to diversify is a fiduciary one. However, the court said, plaintiffs would have to clear a "high evidentiary hurdle" to overcome ERISA's presumption in favor of investing in company stock in an ESOP.

In *In re Goodyear Tire & Rubber,* No. 5:03-cv-2182 (N.D. Ohio July 6, 2006), a district court took the side of plaintiffs, ruling that if fiduciaries know or should have known about impending pressure on the stock due to accounting irregularities soon to be disclosed, they should have taken action to reduce company stock holdings. But in *Pedraza v. Coca-Cola Company,* No. 1:05-cv-1256ODE (N.D. Ga. Sept. 9, 2006), a district court held that fiduciaries could continue to hold company stock in an ESOP even though there had been a 33% drop in share value. The court ruled that removing the shares from the ESOP would be required only if the company were "on the brink of collapse."

While there are differences among these cases and the DOL's position, certain common themes emerge:

1. If employees are investing in company stock, fiduciaries have an affirmative responsibility to provide them with information that is timely and objective, although there is disagreement about what to do with information that, if released, could drive down the stock price (this is not an issue for closely companies, however).

2. If there is good reason to believe the stock price will fall relative to other investment opportunities, fiduciaries must be able to document that holding on to company stock is nonetheless in the best interests of plan participants as participants, not simply as employees.

3. Appointing fiduciaries are responsible to make sure the fiduciaries are properly qualified and informed (and, as in the remarkable case of Enron's alleged failure to appoint an ESOP trustee, that there actually is a designated fiduciary).

4. When there is a conflict, the interests of plan participants as participants must always prevail over other corporate interests or interests over other owners. This "golden rule" of employee ownership, if faithfully followed, will keep the vast majority of ownership plans out of court and out of trouble.

CHAPTER FIVE

Who Should Be the Fiduciary?

Corey Rosen

After reading the other chapters in this book, it's tempting to conclude that every company needs an independent ESOP fiduciary. After all, the issues are so complex and the potentially liability so great. But, of course, the issue is not so simple. All that expertise and risk sharing comes at a cost. Independent fiduciaries charge for their time, of course, but much of the cost is for the risk involved. Fiduciaries get sued, independent or not. In fact, some of the major players in this market have dropped out in recent years because they were getting sued too much. Arguably, most of these transactions were ones in which the fiduciary sanctioned deals that were, at best, on the edge of acceptability and, at worst, outright egregious. Very few ESOPs set up and run with good intentions and good advice end up in court, but the threat is enough to make the potential risk of being an independent fiduciary expensive. As a result, independent fiduciaries can charge tens of thousands of dollars annually. Fees vary widely depending on the size of the company and the plan (there is more financial risk if there are more participants and assets), the complexity of the transaction, and the tasks required (it is less risky to approve an annual valuation than to approve a complex, multi-investor leveraged transaction, for instance). Aside from cost, there is the issue of control. If the fiduciary is not genuinely independent, then hiring an outside trustee does little to reduce the risk for whatever individual or group in the company who is actually acting as the fiduciary.

Yet that independence could mean the fiduciary makes decisions the company's leadership does not like. So given all this, do you still really need an independent fiduciary? Like most answers to ESOP questions, the answer to this one is "it depends."

Understand, of course, that these are only my own views. I am not an attorney or any other kind of ESOP professional, and, no doubt, some professionals will not agree with some or all of what I say. Most would be a good deal more cautious on this issue, and their concerns deserve hearing. But over my 25 years or so in this field, certain themes have emerged that seem to provide reasonable guidance.

The Issue of Cost

Let's face it. There are some companies who, faced with an annual cost of, say $30,000 (just an arbitrary number; it could be much less or more), are just not going to hire an independent fiduciary, even if they really can afford it. With all the other ESOP costs, this may be the one that pushes leadership over the edge and makes them say "just forget the whole thing!" Unless these ESOPs are being set up for less than legitimate reasons, not doing an ESOP because a fiduciary costs too much is probably not a wise choice. Just go ahead an create an internal fiduciary or fiduciaries—but see below about what to do when you have them. There are other companies where the cost is more critical, especially smaller companies. The amount paid a fiduciary might mean the difference between hiring another person or not or paying a small profit sharing check. Here too, this should probably not be a reason in itself not to do an ESOP; just designate an insider as trustee.

The Issue of Independence

My suspicions are immediately raised when someone says they don't want an independent fiduciary simply because they do not want to cede control over the plan. It's an understandable concern. Maybe the fiduciary will sell the company from out under you, claiming the acquirer, who you've been working against all your life, is offering a great price. Or maybe the independent fiduciary will decide your time as CEO should come to an end. These fears are understandable, but they aren't realistic in light of experience. To my knowledge, not a single company has been sold by an independent fiduciary when the management of the company opposed it. I also don't know of any independent fiduciaries throwing out management. In fact, there are actually cases of inside fiduciaries doing both of these things, albeit they are very unusual. Independent fiduciaries want to work cooperatively with company leadership when they can, and it appears that they almost always do.

Much of this may be a self-fulfilling prophecy. Companies that hire independent fiduciaries are probably confident that if the ESOP is run according to the spirit and letter of the law, they have nothing to fear. So the reason I become suspicious about the independence argument is that I wonder if management really has something up its sleeve a little dicey. The answer is probably no, but the record shows that having an independent trustee really isn't that much of a threat, so fear of independence probably is not a good argument.

What an Independent Fiduciary Provides

An independent fiduciary does add a lot of benefits:

1. If you are sued, an independent fiduciary is no guarantee of victory, but it helps in two ways. First, it shows the court that you took the ESOP seriously and tried to do the right thing. Second, the fiduciary's expertise and experience will be an enormous asset in winning the lawsuit.
2. More important, a well-qualified independent fiduciary will help you stay out of court to begin with by red-flagging potential conflicts and problems and by making sure the plan is run properly.
3. A good independent fiduciary will be able to provide valuable advice on deal structuring, communications, plan administration, valuation, and other issues. True, you are hiring experts for all of these things, but the independent fiduciary's expertise and experience can be helpful in advising company leadership even on issues that are not directly fiduciary decisions.
4. An independent trustee may provide employees with a greater sense of comfort that the plan is being run for their benefit.

5. If there is an acquisition, an independent trustee's experience can be invaluable not only in making sure it meets the legal guidelines required but also in getting the best deal for the participants. That benefits everyone, including owners outside the ESOP, who probably get the same price.
6. If the goal is to prevent an unwanted takeover, an independent fiduciary may seem to increase the risk, as it must look solely to the financial interests of participants as participants, not as employees (so must any fiduciary, of course, but the reality is that an inside fiduciary is human, and the loss of employment colors judgment). That's a risk, but, on the other hand, if the fiduciary is persuaded this is not a good deal in the long run, it will be a lot harder for the acquirer to win in court, if it goes that far. In practice, however, unwanted ESOP acquisitions are more the stuff of discussion than occurrence, no matter who the fiduciary is.

What to Look for in an Independent Fiduciary

You may still decide, as most ESOPs do, to have an internal fiduciary. If so, skip this section and go to the one on who an internal fiduciary should be. But if you do decide to hire an independent fiduciary, here are some things to look for.

1. Price: It will appear towards the bottom when advisors make their lists, but the reality is that it's near the top for most companies. But be sure to compare apples to apples. You are paying for three things: the specific services provided (these will vary), the expertise and reputation of the fiduciary, and the risk to which you are exposing the fiduciary.
2. Experience: Ask for a list of ESOP client engagements, including a description of services provided.
3. Involvement in professional organizations: No reputable ESOP trustee would not be a member of the NCEO and/or (preferably and) the ESOP Association. It's even better if they have spoken at their meetings and/or written for their publications. They should also be involved in continuing education on ERISA-related issues.

4. Ability to understand your transaction: Test drive a trustee by providing an overview of the transaction and interviewing them about how they would deal with issues involved. If you have a staged ESOP transaction for instance (where the ESOP is buying out a chunk of stock, then another chunk later), see how they approach issues of paying a control price in all transactions. If you have additional investors, find out how they would approach equity allocation between the ESOP and the investors.

5. Obtain a detailed engagement proposal: This should provide you with detail on what they would do, how much it would cost, and which staff person would be involved. Also obtain a due diligence checklist you can review with them.

6. If you are relying on the trustee to hire other advisors in the transaction, find out who these may be: These should be people who can demonstrate competence and experience. Lots of people say they have done ESOPs, but relatively few have done very many.

Using an Independent Fiduciary Only for Certain Issues

A common compromise is to hire an independent fiduciary when there is an issue that presents potential conflicts or levels of complexity beyond what internal trustees comfortably can handle. For instance, an independent fiduciary could be hired just to make a decision on whether or how to deal with an acquisition proposal or to make a large transaction from an existing owner. For normal plan operations, an internal fiduciary would be used.

Selecting an Internal Fiduciary

If your company will have an internal fiduciary, it's easiest to start by saying who should not be the ESOP fiduciary—anyone selling stock to the ESOP. That person has an inherent conflict of interest. Should the seller run from one side of the table to represent the employees then the other side to be the seller when the sale terms are set? If an ESOP ends up in court, having the seller as the fiduciary is already two strikes against you.

In many companies, the fiduciary is an officer or group of officers of the company. There is still an issue here in that these people's jobs may be dependent on the good will of a seller if the seller still is acting in a management or board capacity. It is therefore especially important that these fiduciaries follow the proper steps to get qualified, independent advice and to carefully consider their actions in light of what ERISA and fair dealing with the plan require. On the other hand, their familiarity with company financial data and overall corporate strategy is a plus.

Finally, in some companies, an ESOP fiduciary committee is created with management and nonmanagement employees represented. This issue is covered in detail in the chapter by Tony Mathews in this book.

Whatever insider is the trustee, it is essential that this person or these people become steeped in ESOP law and lore. They need to read the books, go to the meetings, read the newsletters. The more they understand the details of their responsibility, the less likely they are to get themselves and the company in trouble. If inside fiduciaries cannot or will not make this effort, then hiring an independent fiduciary is imperative.

CHAPTER SIX

Notes to In-House Employee Fiduciaries

Anthony Mathews

Through the early years of ESOP development, the fiduciary teams set up by most ESOP companies rested on the skill of professional fiduciaries. It usually went without saying that the trustee of the ESOP would be a bank or trust company, and, if not, then virtually every non-institutional trustee of an ESOP was either a principal of the company (often the founder or selling shareholders) or a high-ranking executive or group of executives. Some of these fiduciary decisions were good ideas and some were not, but at least all of the people involved could be presumed to be knowledgeable about business in general or the ESOP business in particular and presumably could take on that responsibility with their eyes wide open.

As the ESOP community has matured, we have seen an increase in involvement in the fiduciary process at ever-broader levels within ESOP companies. Today I'd estimate that something better than half of my ESOP clients have individual trustees or boards of trustees comprised of high-ranking employees of the company, or, in some cases, ESOP committees that include, at least in part, people we would normally refer to as "rank and file." Don't get me wrong; I think this is wonderful. I think it signals, perhaps, a maturity in the concept of employee ownership as a capital structure that may make it possible for "employee owned" to take its rightful place beside "publicly traded" and "closely held" as a legitimate, permanent alternative for the capital ownership of an operating company rather than just the tax-efficient, transitional business-succession vehicle it has largely been to date. But that's another story. The point is that we are seeing large numbers of people involved in the management of ESOPs (and, by extension, of the companies they own) who would not normally find themselves in that position. This brief chapter is for that group of brave souls, usually called "in-house" or "non-professional" fiduciaries.

Recently, I was at an ESOP seminar attended by representatives from a number of companies. Our topic was "Corporate Governance in an ESOP Company," and all the attendees were eagerly assembled to get the latest information on this important subject. Through the course of the morning session, a lot of questions were discussed, most of which were very basic, such as "What does a board of directors do?", "Who really runs an ESOP company?", and even "What is a fiduciary?" We wound up having a long and very detailed discussion of the role of the fiduciary, who is one and who is not one, which seemed to come as new information to most of the people present. As we were about to break for lunch, I finally remembered to do something I always try to do at these kinds of events. I asked the people in the room to identify their roles in their ESOP companies so that we could structure the afternoon portion of the session more to their interests.

To tell you the truth, I was a bit stunned by the result. When I asked if there were any trustees or ESOP committee members in the audience, most of the people in the room raised their hands. I was stunned because it was clear from the first part of the meeting that most of these folks had only the most superficial understanding of what that means, and worse yet, it seemed pretty clear to me that at least some of the people in that category didn't even realize that we had been talking about them all morning.

I guess I shouldn't have been so stunned. More than once I have heard or been in conversations with people I know to be fiduciaries but who use words like "they" in reference to fiduciary risks and liabilities when the pronoun really ought to land a lot closer to home.

Are You a Fiduciary?

You might assume that because you are not a trustee, you are not a fiduciary. Alas, that may not be true. If you make decisions concerning plan operations that affect either plan assets or the benefits provided to participants, or you cause someone else to make a particular decision that affects assets or benefits, then you will probably be considered a fiduciary with regard to those decisions. And if the decisions turn out to be wrong, you might be personally liable to make them right. So if you are a member of an ESOP committee, depending on what the committee does, you may well be (I'd even say you are likely to be) a fiduciary, at least some of the time. See the first chapter in this book for more details on this. If you are on a board of trustees, you are absolutely a fiduciary whenever you act in that capacity.

So, here's the real shock: When we are talking about fiduciary liability, fiduciary responsibility, and all that scary stuff . . . it's about you! I'm sure you are confident in the idea that you are a responsible and honest person who will act honorably in every situation. Isn't that enough? I wish it were.

A reasonable paraphrase from the court's decision in one of the most famous early ESOP court cases (*Donovan v. Cunnigham*, 715 F.2d 1455 (5th Cir., 1983) tells the story. The case turned on the fact that the fiduciary of an ESOP allowed some transactions to occur on the basis of a valuation that was clearly stale (about 18 months old) and equally clearly incorrect (it was based on a number of assumptions about business success that had not borne out). To the fiduciary's defense that he had been relying in absolute good faith on the valuation, and his assertion that he was not equipped to know if it was correct or not, the judge replied: "A pure heart and an empty head are not enough." More recent court cases have further expanded this responsibility, even to the extent of limiting the degree to which an ESOP company can indemnify fiduciaries. When all is said and done, it is necessary to act in good faith, but it is not enough to just mean well. If you are going to be successful as a fiduciary, you also have to know enough to be able to do well too.

Anyway, brave soul, if you find yourself in this position, here are a few words of advice from someone who has been around long enough to have seen a lot of mistakes made.

Advice for In-House Fiduciaries

Don't be shy; you need information about the company to do your job, and you have a right to it.

You will often have heard ESOP professionals (even me) refer to that fact that the disclosure requirements placed on an ESOP sponsor are minimal. As ESOP sponsors, we are not obligated to distribute information related to company finances and so forth to employees and in many cases, in fact, it is not even a good idea to do so. Having said that, please note: this does not apply to trustees. Trustees have a right to all the financial information shareholders are entitled to and they have an obligation to act on it. Obviously, then, if you are to serve as a trustee, you should be privy at least to all the financial information that any other shareholder would be entitled to receive, literally. That means that if you are a trustee of an ESOP that owns 100% of a company, you are entitled to everything. If you are trustee of a smaller, minority-owner ESOP, you may be entitled to less (but you nonetheless may need more to make good decisions, and you should insist on getting it). Whatever the circumstances, you should be receiving all the information you are entitled to, and if you are not, you must ask for it. Beyond that, if something doesn't make sense to you, then it must be explained to your satisfaction.

Don't take this job lightly. You have an obligation to prepare yourself to deal with the entire range of business and other related information you receive.

If you are serving as the trustee of an ESOP, you are serving in the place of an owner of your company, and you are responsible to protect the best interests of that owner. That means that you need to see and understand all the reports that illustrate the health of your charge. If financial statements give you a headache (and, God knows, they give me one), you'll just have to get over it. It's your job to be able to read and interpret those reports.

You need to know the difference between an income statement and a balance sheet (at least as much as the typical associate CPA does, anyway). Oh, don't despair totally. You needn't solve the age-old conundrum, "Why is this debit such a positive thing while this credit is just awful?" You just need to understand what the underlying results represent. And you need to know what all these arcane items mean to the company and its success or failure.

You ought to be privy to your company's strategic and business plans (if not involved in generating them). And you ought to be informed about any significant matter related to the growth or operation of the business.

I could go on, but you get the idea. There is a basic (albeit complex and often unnecessarily obscure) language of business, and you have to learn to speak it at least as well as, for example, you'd need to speak Spanish to get a hotel room in Cozumel.

There are several good programs out there, such as the Great Game of Business (www.greatgame.com) and the NCEO *Front-Line Finance* manual, as well as a growing number of courses offered by associations and even universities around the country that you can use to get a start on that, and you can, and should, insist on getting whatever training you need to feel comfortable that you understand what you are looking at.

Develop the several specific skills particular to the roles of the trustee and fiduciary.

Probably the most important function of an ESOP fiduciary is to receive, approve, and implement the annual independent valuation. If you have ever looked through one of these wonderfully informative works (and we sincerely hope you have), you will know that they are filled to the covers with fantastic and often arcane bits—financial statements and projections; industry analyses; data related to comparable public companies; extensive narratives on various valuation methodologies used; summaries of ratios to be applied to your data; summaries of findings based on your data; explanations of weighting, if any; descriptions of relevant assumptions applied to determine your estimate of value; as well as the rationale for and description of all the post-value adjusters (such as minority discounts or control premiums, marketability discounts, etc.).

If you have glazed over just reading the litany, you have my sympathy, but that doesn't let you off the hook. All of those things go into making up the appraisal and that controls the benefits and virtually all the important functions you perform. And it is your responsibility to determine if it has been correctly done or not. Well, how do you plan to do that if you don't read and understand it, or if you don't understand the financial instruments upon which the valuation is based?

A fiduciary also might be called upon to oversee a participant vote. As a trustee or fiduciary, if an issue arises that calls for participants to give you voting instructions, it will fall to you to explain the corporate issue at stake, to understand it yourself, and perhaps to advise participants as to what course you would recommend. You will need to make sure people get the information they need (and the law requires) to make a decision. You also will have responsibility for making sure the plan is operated properly—that people get their distributions on time, that distributions are not made in a discrimantory fashion, that plan assets are not improperly used to pay plan expenses, and that many other details described elsewhere in this book are attended to. In what may be the most difficult situation, you may have to make decisions about whether to continue to invest in company stock, to buy more shares, or even to sell the company.

There are avenues you can take to fill these gaps. First, you ought to insist on attending every ESOP function you can, and you ought to go to every session you can on fiduciary responsibilities, hang out with other in-house fiduciaries, and compare notes.

Also, you should never be shy about using your professionals as support. One often hears laments over the cost of advice in these matters: "I just hate to pay those high hourly rates for advice. We are honorable people who will make the right decisions. Why can't we just do what's right?" Well, I'm afraid that might be a lot like having your brain tumor removed by your gardener because he's a really great guy, honest as the day is long, seems to know a lot about sharp stuff, and he's very inexpensive. If you insist on being a fiduciary, you owe it to yourself (to say nothing of the little dears who are counting on you not to squander the estate on a simple mistake) to do it with the best information and advice you can get. A few hundred dollars for advice now is more than worth offsetting thousands in legal fees for defense later.

Don't let meetings be dominated by a single voice: running an ESOP is a group activity.

It is pretty common for boards of trustees in small companies, in all sincerity and with their good hearts pumping like crazy, to reduce themselves to rubber stamps. As a result of an inclination to collegiality or because of the sheer dominance of a single personality, many fiduciary groups become really just reflections of one (or, at least, less than all) of the voices.

If you are a member of the board of trustees, then you are a trustee. Your voice is critical to the process, and, more to our point here, you are obligated to make it heard. A legal premise called "joint and several" liability means that all members of a group can sometimes be responsible for the acts of all the other members of the group. That is the case with your ESOP board of trustees. You might not get your way about things, but there should, at least, be a record of what you thought about them as you went along.

Be organized. And, if you can't, get someone on the board who is.

You'll have a ton of meetings and discussions in your tenure as a trustee, and it is important that there be a record of, at least, all of the decisions you have made and why. Actions taken at meetings will be lost before you can get to your car in the parking lot unless they are recorded and kept in some organized and accessible manner. I'm not good enough at this myself to tell you any more, but you know what I'm talking about. And I'm sure you can handle it.

Remember this is not just a legal technical function; it is a group effort to accomplish a complex and sometimes emotionally charged action.

Don't forget that at the core of all these events there are people. We are all sometimes well-informed and sometimes ignorant. We are all selfish from time to time, and we are often generous as well. We are all stupid and wise—well, most of us are, anyway. Take that into account and try to start any process from the perspective that there are usually no bad people involved in these things. And, in any interaction, ultimately, you can't go wrong just saying what's true.

There is really great stuff elsewhere in this book to fill in all the details about what you need to know as a fiduciary. But if all this stuff scares you, remember the role is voluntary. You don't have to accept it, and I, for one, don't think any the less of someone who thinks through this process and decides against taking it on. There is no shame in that. If you do decide to take in on though, I hope you will take it seriously enough to do it well, and I hope this helps you, at least a bit, in that pursuit.

CHAPTER SEVEN

Don't Be Fooled: Sarbanes-Oxley Applies to Private ESOP Companies

Helen Morrison
Colleen Helmer
Michael Falk

The Sarbanes-Oxley Act of 2002, the celebrated federal corporate governance legislation, has had a broad impact. Congress passed the law (somewhat hastily) following an unprecedented number of scandals at companies whose names are now synonymous with corporate corruption and misdeeds: Enron, WorldCom, and Tyco, to name a few. The aim of the act is to make public companies more accountable to their public investors and thereby increase public confidence.

Congress is not the only governmental or rulemaking body focused on improving corporate governance and assuring that executive compensation levels are appropriate. The Securities and Exchange Commission (SEC) issued regulations interpreting provisions of Sarbanes-Oxley regarding executive compensation, executive stock sales, audit requirements, and other areas. The New York Stock Exchange (NYSE) and the Nasdaq issued rules regarding the composition of boards of directors and requiring shareholder approval for certain management and employee stock plans. These rules are designed to improve the quality of board oversight and to limit excessive management compensation. The Financial Accounting Standards Board (FASB) issued rules requiring the expensing of stock options. The intent of these rules is to make companies more accurately report their compensation expenses and to assure that management teams have the proper compensation incentives.

Finally, Institutional Shareholder Services (ISS) and other corporate watchdog groups have taken a prominent role in influencing public company investors and existing shareholders by publishing report cards that rate companies based on their corporate governance performance. These groups have developed strict criteria for best practices and regularly publish the names of those companies that excel and those that don't.

What do Sarbanes-Oxley, the NYSE and Nasdaq rules, and the ISS publications mean to private, ESOP-owned companies? At first glance, the new laws and regulations—and the publicity they've generated—mean nothing because they govern only public companies. Look just a bit closer, however, and it becomes apparent that Sarbanes-Oxley and related SEC regulations have influenced the behavior of private companies, even though they are not subject to the new rules.

Private, ESOP-owned companies cannot ignore the spirit of Sarbanes-Oxley. As discussed in this chapter, ESOP-owned companies are more similar to public companies than they are to closely held private companies. Sarbanes-Oxley may directly govern only public companies, but it sets the federal standard for accepted governance practices for all companies. It should be understood and considered.

Why Are ESOP-Owned Companies More Like Public Companies?

Let's consider the spectrum of public companies to private companies. At one end is the widely held public company. Its board of directors oversees the management of the business in order to enhance shareholder value. The board's actions have an impact on a broad ownership population. With the enactment of Sarbanes-Oxley, public companies are now required to comply with extensive and often costly governance requirements in order to assure that the directors and managers are properly accountable to the shareholders.

At the other end of spectrum is a private company that is owned by a single shareholder who is the president, CEO, and sole member of the board of directors. This person could operate the businesses with complete disregard of acceptable governance and executive compensation best practices, and would argue that he himself is the only person who is hurt by a loss of share value. Even less closely held private companies are not subject to Sarbanes-Oxley or any of the other public company corporate governance regulations. Consequently, private owners have greater freedom to operate their businesses as they choose.

We argue that on this spectrum, ESOP companies are much closer to public companies than to other private companies. The boards of directors and managers of ESOP-owned companies are responsible for preserving and enhancing share value for a broad-based group, which includes the ESOP participants and beneficiaries, who have a beneficial interest in the company through their ESOP accounts. Unlike the sole owner of a private business, the directors and managers of an ESOP-owned company are accountable to a broad group of owners. Failure to operate the business for the benefit of all current and future stakeholders may result in personal liability.

Good corporate governance has two significant benefits for public and private ESOP-owned companies alike. First, companies that use governance best-practices tend to outperform their competition. In a recent study, McKinsey & Company found a 12% to 14% premium on stock value for companies with good governance practices (e.g., those in which a majority of directors are independent, managers must submit to review and oversight, and other practices defined in the study are followed).[1] In addition, the study found that 60% of investors would avoid companies with "poor" governance, and 57% of investors rate corporate governance equal to or higher in importance than financial reporting.

The adoption of good corporate governance practices also may protect an ESOP company from potential liability under the Employee Retirement Income Security Act of 1974 (ERISA), as amended. An ESOP is a retirement benefit plan that is subject to the fiduciary rules and other requirements of ERISA. ESOP fiduciaries have the responsibility under ERISA to act prudently and for the exclusive benefit of participants and their beneficiaries. Many ESOP trustees and other fiduciaries believe that to act prudently in today's climate is to monitor closely and understand what is going on in the public company arena—by knowing the particulars of Sarbanes-Oxley and the spirit behind it and by understanding

---

1. McKinsey & Company's Global Opinion Survey, 2002.

other public-company regulations—and to incorporate these principles into their business operations.[2]

This chapter will focus on a few of the key provisions of Sarbanes-Oxley that have applicability to private, ESOP-owned companies.

The Sarbanes-Oxley Answer to Certain Corporate Issues

The public outrage generated by the Enron and other corporate scandals pressured Congress to do something—and quickly. Lawmakers hustled to cobble together legislation to more closely oversee public companies and the professionals who audit them. Congress hoped to restore public confidence in the financial reporting process and to increase the accuracy of the financial statements produced by the companies, as attested to by outside auditors and ultimately relied on by investors. As a result, much of Sarbanes-Oxley focuses on deterring corporate wrongdoing and punishing those who act inappropriately.

Specifically, Sarbanes-Oxley's provisions regarding assessing an organization's culture and tightening up internal controls require management to exercise value-based judgment meant to cultivate good corporate citizenship. The enhanced audit committee requirements force corporations to own up to rather than cover up the inevitable transgressions. And, finally, the civil and criminal penalty provisions provide the teeth necessary to deter would-be corporate looters from profiting at shareholders' expense. Collectively, these provisions provide a strong foundation from which any company can build a robust corporate gov-

---

2. In its amicus brief in the Enron ERISA litigation (*Tittle vs. Enron*), the Department of Labor (DOL) took the position that directors and certain senior managers may be held responsible as ERISA fiduciaries with respect to an ESOP or other ERISA plan that holds employer securities. The DOL stated that certain Enron directors and officers who served on Enron's ESOP plan administration committee had the fiduciary responsibility to oversee the ESOP and to disclose material information. In the wake of the Enron litigation and other ERISA actions, directors and officers of ESOP companies may be more vulnerable to fiduciary liability. Compliance with good corporate governance practices may not be a perfect defense to a claim that an officer or director breached his or her fiduciary duty, but it certainly will improve the chances of success.

ernance structure able to withstand what is certain to be an enhanced level of scrutiny in the post-Enron era.

Tone at the Top

Even the best-controlled company is not immune from corporate fraud. The key to good governance exists not in the laws passed by Congress or in the rules promulgated by government agencies, but in the values espoused by the company and the degree to which such values are embraced by the company's executives. In fact, the failures that resulted in the passage of Sarbanes-Oxley (and those that subsequently have surfaced in the headlines on a shockingly frequent basis) can all be traced to a single common malady—the failure to institute an ethical culture.

Take WorldCom, for example. Whatever one's view of Bernie Ebbers' personal involvement in the financial fraud that has been disclosed, it is apparent that he promoted, or at minimum permitted, a culture of making the numbers at all costs.

The cultural and ethical climate of a corporation starts at the top and pervades the entire organization. Those who set the policy also set the tone and, ultimately, the values of the organization. This concept, referred to as the "tone at the top," can foster and encourage ethical corporate behavior or, as has been documented widely and in painful detail, it can spark an organization's demise.

Although Congress cannot legislate ethics, it can impose requirements designed to encourage a culture of honesty and openness. Two specific sections of Sarbanes-Oxley address this notion. Section 407 requires a public company to disclose whether it has a written code of ethics that applies to its principal executive officer, financial officer, accounting officer or controller, and people performing similar functions. Section 407 defines a code of ethics as written standards that are reasonably necessary to deter wrongdoing and promote:

- honest and ethical conduct, including the ethical handling of actual or apparent conflicts of interest between personal and professional relationships;
- full, fair, accurate, timely, and understandable disclosure in the periodic reports required to be filed by the issuer; and
- compliance with applicable governmental rules and regulations.

A company without an existing code of ethics is not required to write one, nor is a company with an existing code that does not meet the definition described above required to amend it. However, in both cases, the company must disclose in its annual report filed with the SEC the reason why it doesn't meet the standards. Thus, given the adverse reaction likely to follow such an admission, it would seem that most companies will opt either to create new codes of ethics or enhance their existing codes to satisfy the requirements of Section 407.

The existence of a written code of ethics, while a step in the right direction, does not automatically guarantee an ethical corporate environment. By way of hackneyed example, Enron had an ethics code. But, as one critic observed, "at Enron, ethics was simply a piece of paper with three Ps—print, post (in the company lunch room), and then pray that something is actually going to happen."[3] So just as important as (and some would argue, even more important than) a written code of ethics, is a management team that exemplifies ethical behavior. That is, the code of ethics must be put into action, and the action must start at the top. The next section addresses management's responsibility to assess internal controls in the context of Section 404 of Sarbanes-Oxley.

Internal Control

The CFO of Tyco paid himself an unauthorized bonus of $8 million. Why and how did he do this? Because he could. Tyco did not have appropriate internal controls to monitor management's behavior. Without adequate controls, even good people may do bad things.

Sarbanes-Oxley is designed to improve corporate controls. Section 404 requires management to annually:

- state its responsibility for establishing and maintaining adequate internal control over financial reporting;
- identify the framework used to evaluate the effectiveness of internal control over financial reporting;

---

3. Heesun Wee, "Corporate Ethics: Right Makes Might," *Business Week Online*, April 11, 2002, quoting Stuart Gilman, president of the Ethics Resource Center in Washington, D.C.

- assess the effectiveness of the company's internal controls over financial reporting as of year-end; and
- state that its auditor has issued an attestation report on management's assessment.

Section 302, a separate but related provision, requires CEOs and CFOs to personally certify that disclosure controls and procedures have been implemented and evaluated.

Before Sarbanes-Oxley, most companies did not have direct links from the governance activities of their boards and senior management to the control activities of the organization. But now, because the law requires top executives to state, for the record, how well their internal control structures are functioning, establishing such links is crucial to compliance.[4] Thus, executives can no longer rely on the "I didn't know" defense. Accountability is the new order of the day.

Evaluating the effectiveness of internal controls over financial reporting sounds, to most non-auditors, ominous and daunting. However, most public and private companies, whether they realize it or not, already have in place some type of internal control structure. Sarbanes-Oxley requires each company to formally identify a control framework and evaluate its effectiveness related to financial reporting. The most dominant control framework used in the United States was developed by the Committee of Sponsoring Organizations of the Treadway Commission and is commonly referred to as "COSO." This framework comprises five interrelated components: control environment, risk assessment, control activities, information and communication, and monitoring.

The "control environment" encompasses every facet of the internal control framework—it is the universe in which all of the other elements exist. The control environment includes the intangibles that make up the company's culture and derives much of its strength from the tone established by the company's board and executives.[5] A detailed discussion of the effectiveness of a company's controls in the context of the

---

4. *Moving Forward–A Guide to Improving Corporate Governance Through Effective Internal Control, A Response to Sarbanes-Oxley,* Deloitte & Touche, January 2003, p. 7.
5. Id. at 15.

entire COSO framework is beyond the scope of this chapter. However, effectiveness ultimately depends on the nature of the control environment.

How receptive is management to bad news? How important is making your sales targets? What behavior is rewarded by your supervisor? What behavior is not tolerated? Is your boss ethical? Are your co-workers ethical? Are you ethical? The answers to these and similar questions will provide an organization with a preliminary sketch of its control environment. Note that the makeup of the audience from which answers to these questions are solicited will directly affect the results. Just as one would expect different results from a teacher completing a self-evaluation versus students performing a teacher evaluation, so too, will the complete and accurate picture of the control environment depend upon the differing (yet equally valid) perspectives of executives, managers, and staff at all levels.

Codes of ethics and positive tones at the top are likely familiar concepts to many ESOP-owned companies. But structured internal control systems for financial reporting may be new for private ESOP companies. Implementation of internal controls can only improve the quality and accuracy of a company's financial statements and ultimately its economic performance.

Audit Committee Responsibilities

Section 301 of Sarbanes-Oxley, which amends Section 10A of the Securities Exchange Act of 1934, adds the following provisions related to enhanced audit committee responsibilities:

- The audit committee is directly responsible for the appointment, compensation, and oversight of the work of any registered public accounting firm employed by the company to perform audit services (including the resolution of disagreements between management and the auditor regarding financial reporting), and the accounting firm is required to report directly to the audit committee.
- Each member of the audit committee must be an "independent" director, which means that she may not (other than in her capacity as a member of the audit committee, the board of directors, or any

other board committee) accept any consulting, advisory or other compensatory fee, or be affiliated with the company or any of its subsidiaries.

Additionally, Section 406 of Sarbanes-Oxley requires the audit committee to have at least one member who is a "financial expert" (and if it does not, it must disclose the reason why). Generally, this expert understands generally accepted accounting principles and their applicability to accounting for estimates, accruals and reserves; has experience analyzing financial statements comparable to the company's; and understands internal controls, procedures for financial reporting, and audit committee functions.

These audit committee requirements have been criticized as overly restrictive and expensive. Companies are concerned about the cost of identifying and engaging an independent audit committee member who satisfies the narrow definition of a "financial expert." Private, ESOP-owned companies are fortunate to avoid these specific requirements. But compliance with the spirit of the independent audit committee requirements can enhance the accuracy of a company's financial statements. The independent ESOP appraiser also adds a level of scrutiny that does not exist for other private companies.

Executive Accountability

Section 304 of Sarbanes-Oxley provides that if a public company is required to change its financial statements as a result of corporate misconduct, then the CEO and CFO must return any bonus or other incentive compensation received for the year following the misstatement and must forfeit any profits realized from any stock sales during the period.

Executive Compensation

An underlying theme of Sarbanes-Oxley and other proposed legislation and regulations is the concern that executives are receiving excessive compensation without regard to their companies' performance. The trend is to assure that the level and form of executive compensation is aligned with the interests of the company and its shareholders. Various remedies have been proposed.

Section 402 of Sarbanes-Oxley prohibits loans to corporate executives. FASB is considering a proposal to require the expensing of stock options. The NYSE and Nasdaq have proposed rules that require a shareholder vote on certain executive compensation programs. Congress has considered legislation to restrict executive deferred compensation. Most importantly, the compensation committees of public companies have heightened awareness that management compensation must enhance, rather than dilute, shareholder value.

Scrutiny of executive compensation is not new for ESOP-owned companies. ESOP fiduciaries were sued in two recent cases—*Delta Star, Inc. v. Patton* and *Eckelkamp v. Beste*—on the grounds that the value of company stock suffered because executives had been excessively compensated. In *Delta Star*, the ESOP participants prevailed based, in part, on the fact that the company's president (who also acted as the ESOP trustee) unilaterally granted himself salary increases, bonuses, and nonqualified retirement benefits without consulting the company's other board members or outside consultants regarding industry standards or the proper criteria to be used to establish his compensation. In *Eckelkamp*, the ESOP trustee prevailed thanks, in part, to a compensation structure that the court found to be well-documented and well-designed. Management's compensation was found to be competitive with the industry, reflective of company performance, and aligned with the interests of employees and other shareholders.

Due to heightened attention to the level and form of executive compensation, ESOP companies and plan fiduciaries are cautioned to give particular attention the compensation packages of key management employees.

Penalties

Title IX of Sarbanes-Oxley established the "White Collar Crime Penalty Enhancement Act of 2002." Section 906 provides that any person convicted of knowingly violating the certification requirements of Section 302 will be fined up to $1 million, imprisoned for up to 10 years, or both. The same section further provides that any person who "willfully" violates the certification requirement will be fined up to $5 million, imprisoned for up to 20 years, or both.

Section 806 of Sarbanes-Oxley protects employees of publicly traded companies who provide evidence of fraud. The civil remedies include a right to reinstatement, back pay, and damages. The criminal penalty provision makes it a felony to retaliate against a protected whistleblower.

For the most audacious offenders, Sarbanes-Oxley also imposes criminal penalties on any person "(i) who knowingly alters, destroys, mutilates, conceals, covers up, or falsifies with the intent to impede, obstruct, or influence the investigation or administration of any matter within the jurisdiction of any department or agency of the U.S. (fines, imprisonment for up to 20 years or both), or (ii) who defrauds shareholders of publicly traded companies (fines, imprisonment for up to 25 years or both)."

The penalties for violating the provisions of Sarbanes-Oxley are severe. Private ESOP companies are not directly subject to these penalties. However, failure to comply with the spirit behind the control requirements, audit independence, and executive accountability provisions of Sarbanes-Oxley can result in other types of consequences from financial underperformance to ERISA fiduciary liability.

Conclusion

By implementing the internal control, independent audit review, and executive accountability provisions of Sarbanes-Oxley, ESOP companies are less likely to face ERISA liability for breach of a fiduciary duty to the ESOP, and equally importantly may improve their financial performance.

ESOP companies, like all other companies, are governed by boards of directors, managers, and shareholders. An ESOP company's governance may also include an ESOP administrative committee. Each of these groups benefits from an understanding and awareness of the spirit and particulars of Sarbanes-Oxley's governance requirements.

The board of directors oversees the governance of the company. It sets broad policies and makes major corporate decisions (e.g., regarding potential acquisitions). The board has the general responsibility for enhancing shareholder value and the specific responsibility for assuring that the company is well-managed by the president and other key managers. In accordance with the dictates and spirit of Sarbanes-Oxley, each

ESOP company should consider appointing an independent director to its board. This independence brings accountability and can help to improve performance.

The board of directors is elected by the shareholders. For a company that has an ESOP shareholder, the ESOP trustee represents the ESOP and votes its shares. An ESOP committee may direct the trustee as to how to vote the shares, or employees may have pass-through voting rights as described elsewhere in this report. The ESOP trustee and the members of the ESOP committee are not directly responsible (in that capacity) for managing the business. However, the trustee and committee members are considered to be fiduciaries under ERISA and can be held personally liable if they are found to have breached their fiduciary duties. This potential for ERISA liability is greatly reduced for any ESOP company that operates in accordance with the Sarbanes-Oxley provisions that require systematic internal controls, independent audit committee review of the financial statements, and accountability of the corporate executives.

The day-to-day business operations of the company are led by the president and other key managers. At first blush, the management team may be less than enthusiastic about adopting the Sarbanes-Oxley system of internal controls and accountability. However, the establishment of appropriate management oversight and good governance arrangements has been shown to improve a company's financial performance. Every management team is happier and more productive if the company is performing well.

CHAPTER EIGHT

ESOP Corporate Governance in a New Era

Helen Morrison

Against the backdrop of increased scrutiny and regulation of corporate governance, ESOP companies find themselves in a unique position. Although closely held ESOP companies are directly subject to recent federal legislation and securities law regulations, they question arises whether they should model their corporate governance practices after the standards being set for public companies.

How do ESOP companies currently govern themselves and how are their practices evolving? This chapter examines the current governance landscape and conveys the findings of Deloitte & Touche's recent survey of 287 ESOP-owned companies conducted with the support of the ESOP Association and the National Center for Employee Ownership (NCEO). This represents an 18% response rate based on the number of e-mail surveys sent. A number of these addresses were no longer valid or otherwise never reached the intended party, or were duplicates, so the actual response rate for surveys that reached the appropriate person would be much higher, probably in the 25% to 30% range. This is a very high rate for such surveys. However, the respondents are drawn from the membership lists of the ESOP Association and the National Center for Employee Ownership, whose membership may not be representative of the ESOP community as a whole on this issue. Presumably, companies who do not join either organization are less likely to be committed to the

ESOP concept and perhaps less concerned about some of the governance issues discussed below. This is only speculation, of course.

Part One: A New Era in Governance

The Sarbanes-Oxley Act of 2002 ("Sarbanes-Oxley" or the "Act") has rewritten the rules for corporate governance in public companies. Sarbanes-Oxley was hastily enacted following corporate scandals at companies like Enron, Tyco and Worldcom. Replete with accounting, disclosure and corporate governance reforms, the Act seeks, in tangible ways, to "repair" the public's lost faith in America's business community.

Behind all the rules and regulations, the Act is simply the government's way of putting legal teeth into the basic precepts of good corporate governance and ethical business practices. Among other statutory requirements, Sarbanes-Oxley requires:

- The adoption of a code of ethics
- CEO and CFO certification for all financial statements
- An independent audit committee and the appointment of a financial "expert" as the chair of the committee
- Increased disclosure requirements, including the disclosure of any significant control deficiencies, material weaknesses, and fraudulent acts
- Establishment of enhanced control procedures

Other quasi-governmental bodies have also issued new rules related to corporate governance and executive compensation. The NYSE and NASDAQ have issued rules governing shareholder voting and board of director membership and practices. Concurrently, the Financial Accounting Standards Board (FASB) issued new rules requiring stock option expensing in order to ensure that executive compensation is more accurately disclosed. In addition, Institutional Shareholder Services (ISS) and other corporate governance watchdogs have developed strict criteria for best governance practices and regularly publish the names of those companies that excel and those that fail to meet the standards.

Impact on ESOP Companies

Is it true that ESOP-owned private companies are exempt from the expensive and burdensome requirements of Sarbanes-Oxley? Can ESOP-owned private companies ignore the current wave of change in corporate governance best practices? The answer is "yes" and "no." Although ESOP-owned private companies are not directly governed by Sarbanes-Oxley and other governance regulations directed at public companies, the spirit and basic requirements of the Act cannot be ignored.

ESOP-owned companies have a unique governance structure. All corporations are governed by three groups: shareholders, a board of directors, and officers and management. The shareholders are the legal owners of all of the stock and have the right to vote their shares to elect the board of directors. The board of directors hires and fires the president/CEO, oversees the work of management, and sets broad policies for the company. Management runs the day-to-day operations of the company.

In an ESOP-owned company, the ESOP trust owns the shares and is represented by the ESOP trustee, who votes the shares. The ESOP trustee has no formal direct interface with management and makes no management decisions, although, in practice, ESOP trustees are frequently corporate officers. If the ESOP trustee does not like a management decision, its sole recourse is to vote to elect new directors to the board of directors. The ESOP trustee may vote the ESOP shares in its sole discretion, based on directions from participants, or as directed by the ESOP committee, if such a committee exists.

On the spectrum from a closely held company in which the actions of CEOs would impact only themselves to a widely held public company, ESOP-owned companies may seem more like the private company. They are not subject to the scrutiny and regulations faced by public companies. However, an ESOP-owned company has a broad number of beneficial employee owners. The actions of company management on shareholder value affect a large group. This makes ESOP-owned companies particularly vulnerable to attacks of breach of fiduciary duty.

How, then, do ESOP-owned companies govern themselves? How large are their boards of directors? Do they seek the expertise of outside directors and, if so, how do they compensate them? How do the ESOP trustee and ESOP committee operate? These are some of the questions posed by Deloitte & Touche to members of the NCEO and the ESOP Association.

Current Practices Among ESOP Companies

In general, the boards of ESOP companies have fewer members than boards for public companies and they tend to meet less frequently. Our study found the average number of directors is six, compared to nine for similar-size public companies. Among 77% of ESOP companies, the board of directors meets four or fewer times per year, as can be seen in table 8-1. In contrast, 44% of public company boards meet six or more times per year.

Table 8-1. Number of Full Board Meetings

	Percentage of ESOP Companies
Less than 4 meetings	36%
4 (e.g., quarterly) meetings	41%
5 meetings	7%
6 meetings	6%
7 to 9 meetings	3%
10 or more meetings	7%

The use of board committees is not extensive in ESOP companies: 30% report having an audit committee, 50% have a compensation committee, and 28% have an executive committee.

The purview of the ESOP board is expansive. The vast majority of survey respondents reported that their boards review many facets of corporate governance.

ESOP boards generally rely on themselves and the CEO to find and recruit new directors. Just over half (54%) use criteria developed by the board to assure the new member has the proper skills and characteristics. Nearly one half (48%) rely on recommendations from the CEO. Just 2% of boards engage a search firm.

Independent Directors

A growing trend for ESOP companies is the addition of independent directors to the board (i.e., independent directors who have no direct financial relationship or current or past employment with the company). Among our respondents, slightly over one half (51%) of ESOP companies currently have one or more independent directors. Nearly one half of these companies report that independent members comprise 50% or more of their entire board, as can be seen in table 8-2.

Table 8-2. Percentage of Board Members That Are Independent

	Percentage of Companies
75% or more	11%
60%–74%	20%
50%–59%	17%
40%–49%	16%
25%–39%	18%
Less than 25%	17%

Approximately 36% of ESOP companies are planning to add independent directors, including 36% of companies that do not currently have independent directors. The vast majority of these companies seek the additional expertise that the properly chosen "outsider" can provide (table 8-3).

Table 8-3. Reasons for Adding Independent Directors

	Percentage of Companies Citing
Seek additional expertise	96%
Provide balance between internal and external viewpoints	69%
Provide needed management skills	24%
Meet regulatory requirements	8%
Other	5%

Interestingly, the expertise these companies seek is not centered on ESOPs. Experience with ESOPs ranks at the bottom of the list of key criteria boards use in selected new independent directors (table 8-4).

Table 8-4. Key Criteria in Selecting Independent Directors

	Percentage of Companies Citing
Technical knowledge (marketing, finance, HR, risk management, etc.)	56%
Industry expertise	42%
Other board experience	27%
ESOP expertise	9%

ESOP Trustees and Committees

The survey found that the ESOP trust is largely governed by management representatives who have broad discretion in voting the ESOP shares. For a significant percentage of companies (39%) an inside officer or employees serves as the ESOP trustee. For 21%, an ESOP committee of management directs the trustee, while in 12% there is a committee with management and non-management employees (table 8-5).

Table 8-5. Who Serves as the ESOP Trustee

	Percentage of Companies
An officer or employee of the company	39%
A committee of management employees	21%
An independent institution (e.g., bank or trust company)	17%
A committee of management and non-management employees	12%
An individual who is not an employee of the company	4%
Other	7%

For nearly two-thirds of companies (64%), the ESOP trustee may vote the ESOP shares in its sole, independent discretion. The responses to this question should not be interpreted to indicate a percentage of respondents who engage an independent institutional trustee or independent fiduciary to serve as (or direct) the ESOP trustee. The responses would indicate that the respondents interpreted the question to ask if the ESOP trustee, whether independent or not, was directed by another individual or committee.

Among those companies where the ESOP trustee does not have sole discretion (36%), the ESOP participants have more authority for a significant number of respondents (table 8-6).

Table 8-6. Who Votes the ESOP Shares If the ESOP Trustee Does Not Have Sole Discretion

	Percentage of Companies
ESOP participants	41%
The board of directors	20%
An administrative committee of officers	19%
President/CEO/other officer	5%
Other	14%

Most of the participating companies (68%) have an ESOP committee whose responsibilities vary. In most cases, the committee must administer the ESOP and also direct the ESOP trustee how to vote the shares.[1] Once again, the board and management have a great deal of influence in selecting committee members (table 8-7).

Table 8-7. How the ESOP Committee Is Selected

	Percentage of companies
By the board	65%
By management	14%
By employee voting	8%
By soliciting volunteers	4%
Employees volunteer, management selects among volunteers	5%
Other	5%

---

1. The term "ESOP committee" has different meanings depending on the company. An "ESOP committee" may mean a legally constituted committee that has the responsibility for voting or directing the vote of the ESOP shares and for plan administration. The term may also be used to describe a committee that has only advisory responsibilities and responsibilities for employee communications. Many companies maintain both types of ESOP committee. The responses to this question should be read with this potential confusion in mind.

In only a very small number of companies do employees have a role in selecting ESOP committee members. These committee members serve for an indefinite term at the majority (55%) of companies.

Employee Involvement

One unique characteristic of ESOP companies is the extent to which their employees are involved in the management of the company and/or receive extensive and frequent information about key management decisions. While a relatively small percentage of ESOP companies (22%) have nonmanagement employees on the board, this practice is almost nonexistent among larger, public companies and even less common in closely held companies. Among these companies with non-management employee board members, the majority (75%) report that employee involvement has not significantly changed board decisions. Companies reporting that employee involvement has altered the performance of the board were four times more likely to say the involvement has had a positive effect on the board's actions.

The majority of ESOP companies regularly provide employees important information regarding the financial and strategic performance of the company. Most of these companies provide this information at least quarterly, as can be seen in table 8-8.

Table 8-8. Information Provided to Employees

Type of Information	Percentage Providing	Annually	Semi-Annually	Quarterly	More Than Quarterly
Financial	72%	24%	10%	30%	36%
Executive Compensation	2%	83%	0%	17%	0%
Strategic/outlook	72%	29%	24%	34%	13%
Corporate performance data	81%	19%	8%	33%	40%
Other	33%	25%	11%	19%	45%

Best Practices for Governance in ESOP Companies

We have already seen that boards at ESOP companies are involved in many facets of management, including strategy review, succession planning, and assessing CEO performance. The role they already play in overseeing these important functions puts them ahead of the game compared to many closely held companies.

As ESOP-owned companies welcome more outside directors to their boardrooms, the need for more formalized governance practices will increase. Boards should put a strong emphasis on the process of good governance in the following areas:

- Leadership and accountability—roles and responsibilities are clearly delineated and performance expectations communicated, assuring that employees have a safe means to report improprieties.
- Communication with company constituencies—employees, customers, and vendors.
- Effective meetings—access to information, not just raw data, beyond what management delivers.
- Expertise—financial, marketing, industry, strategy, human resources, etc.

By being cognizant of the mandates of Sarbanes-Oxley, ESOP-owned companies, like their public counterparts, have an opportunity to forge a new landscape that allows them to achieve new levels of corporate excellence and drive better performance.

Part Two: Board of Directors Compensation in ESOP Companies

Compensation practices vary greatly among ESOP companies. Some primarily use annual retainers, others rely mostly on meeting fees to compensate directors. Few companies use stock compensation. Many companies with only inside directors do not compensate them for board service at all.

The data below are divided by companies with outside directors and those without. Among companies with outside directors, the data are divided by revenue level. To provide a basis for comparison, we have calculated a "total compensation" figure that includes (1) the annual retainer in cash or stock (excludes stock options); (2) board meeting fees, assuming four meetings per year; and (3) committee meeting fees, assuming a director sits on two committees that each meet four times per year.

The compensation levels for the various groups can be seen in the tables below. Note that the rows will not add up to the "total compensation" number. That is because differing percentages of companies use different techniques. So, for instance, in table 8-9, 15% of the 138 respondent companies provide a retainer. The numbers in this column are for that 15% group only. Even for the "total compensation" column, not all companies provide compensation. For instance, in the first table, only 30% of the respondents provide any compensation and the numbers represent only the averages for that 30%. The statistics in each of the columns are arrayed independently from the other columns.

Companies Without Outside Directors

Table 8-9. All Companies Without Outside Directors

	Retainer	Board Meeting Fees	Committee Meeting Fees	Total Compensation
25th percentile	$4,000	$250		$1,300
Median	$7,500	$500		$4,000
Average	$13,700	$1,129		$9,513
75th percentile	$12,800	$1,000		$8,750
Percentage using	15%	17%	NA	30%

n = 138

Companies with Outside Directors

Table 8-10. Less Than $25 Million Revenues

	Retainer	Board Meeting Fees	Committee Meeting Fees	Total Compensation
25th percentile	$1,200	$475	$250	$1,850
Median	$3,125	$1,000	$500	$4,000
Average	$4,293	$1,508	$627	$6,882
75th percentile	$6,000	$1,125	$750	$8,000
Percentage using	36%	64%	21%	82%

$n = 56$

Table 8-11. $25 to $50 Million Revenues

	Retainer	Board Meeting Fees	Committee Meeting Fees	Total Compensation
25th percentile	$3,500	$750	$300	$4,000
Median	$4,500	$1,000	$438	$6,500
Average	$5,317	$2,174	$816	$10,586
75th percentile	$5,500	$1,250	$875	$10,000
Percentage using	41%	68%	22%	89%

$n = 37$

Table 8-12. $50 to $100 Million Revenues

	Retainer	Board Meeting Fees	Committee Meeting Fees	Total Compensation
25th percentile	$4,000	$500	$500	$7,500
Median	$7,250	$1,000	$500	$10,000
Average	$8,988	$1,141	$605	$11,156
75th percentile	$12,750	$1,500	$875	$13,200
Percentage using	62%	73%	38%	96%

$n = 26$

Table 8-13. $100 to $500 Million Revenues

	Retainer	Board Meeting Fees	Committee Meeting Fees	Total Compensation
25th percentile	$6,600	$1,000	$500	$10,900
Median	$10,000	$1,500	$600	$18,400
Average	$11,427	$2,265	$864	$21,605
75th percentile	$14,000	$2,500	$1,100	$27,500
Percentage using	48%	74%	48%	83%

$n = 23$

Table 8-14. Greater Than $500 Million Revenues

	Retainer	Board Meeting Fees	Committee Meeting Fees	Total Compensation
Median	$29,000	$1,550		$45,000
Average	$29,600	$1,550		$45,050
Percentage using	67%	33%	NA	67%

$n = 6$

Appendix: Breakdown of Results by Selected Demographics

Table 8-15. Who the ESOP Trustee Is by Revenue Size and Percentage of Employee Ownership

Who Serves as the ESOP Trustee	Revenue More Than $25 Million	Revenue Less Than $25 Million	Companies 100% ESOP-Owned	Companies Less Than 100% ESOP-Owned
An officer or employee of the company	22%	57%	39%	40.4%
A committee of management employees	25%	17%	18%	23.3%
An independent institution (e.g., bank or trust company)	27%	7%	20%	23.3%
A committee of management and non-management employees	15%	9%	15%	15.3%
An individual who is not an employee of the company	4%	4%	3%	5.8%
Other	7%	7%	6%	8.0%
	$n = 138$	$n = 141$	$n = 119$	$n = 167$

Table 8-16. ESOP Trustee Voting by Revenue Size and Percentage of Employee Ownership

If the ESOP Trustee Does Not Have Sole Discretion, Who Directs the Vote of the ESOP Shares?	Revenue More Than $25 Million	Revenue Less Than $25 Million	Companies 100% ESOP-Owned	Companies Less Than 100% ESOP-Owned
ESOP participants	45%	26%	39%	48%
The board of directors	17%	19%	20%	23%
An administrative committee of officers	17%	17%	16%	25%
President/CEO	4%	6%	7%	5%
	n = 53	n = 40	n = 44	n = 51

Table 8-17. Percentage of Independent Board Members by Revenue Size, Percentage Employee-Owned

Percentage of Independent Board Members	Revenue More Than $25 Million	Revenue Less Than $25 Million	Companies 100% ESOP-Owned	Companies Less Than 100% ESOP-Owned
75% or more	13%	7%	11%	10%
60-74%	22%	17%	20%	20%
50-69%	19%	18%	14%	20%
40-49%	13%	21%	14%	17%
25-39%	20%	17%	23%	15%
< 25%	13%	22%	17%	17%
	n = 89	n = 58	n = 64	n = 86

Demographics of Survey Participants

The 287 ESOP-owned companies that participated in the study represent a wide range of industries. Nearly three-quarters are majority ESOP-owned, with many having 100% ownership by the ESOP. One-half of the respondents have annual revenue of less than $25 million.

Table 8-18. Revenue Breakdown

$1–$3 billion	1%
$500 million–$1 billion	2%
$100–$500 million	12%
$50–$100 million	14%
$25–$50 million	21%
< $25 million	50%

Table 8-19. Percentage of Company Owned by ESOP

100%	42%
75%–99%	12%
51%–74%	15%
41%–50%	6%
31%–40%	9%
11%–30%	11%
< 11%	5%

Table 8-20. Respondents by Industry

Financial	6%
Engineering	3%
Consulting	2%
Healthcare	1%
Telecommunications	1%
Power/Utility	1%
Service	24%
Durable goods/manufacturing	20%
Wholesale/retail	19%
Construction	9%
Non-durable goods manufacturing	8%
Other	7%

CHAPTER NINE

The Role of the Board in ESOP Companies

Cecil Ursprung

When society consisted mainly of hunters and gatherers, were there boards of directors? How about during the agricultural era? Or the Middle Ages, when craftspeople and guilds emerged? Or the merchant era, when countries such as England, France, and Spain were building empires?

Boards arguably go back to medieval times, when societies of independent merchants created boards to govern their joint activities. The concept of boards migrated to some of the early large businesses, as evidenced by board statutes in 1694 for the Bank of England. Colonial and trading companies chartered by the king were required to have boards, a practice that may have influenced the development of boards in the U.S.

But the board as a ubiquitous institution really only emerged in the 19th century. Before that time, most "work organizations" consisted of single individuals who owned and managed their own economic entities. If the same person owns, manages, and produces work output, there is no purpose for a board. Even with the rise of the merchant class and trading activities that extended throughout the world, there was often no need for the oversight function of the board because each voyage was organized by a venturer, and the arrangement was terminated and profits distributed when the voyage was complete.

By the 19th century, as businesses became larger, more complex, and more permanent, ownership and management were more likely to be separate individuals or institutions, and ownership felt a growing need to oversee management. That was especially true when ownership and management were geographically distant. Owner-managed firms often sought boards as well, however, as sources of advice. In the U.S., corporate law has required boards of directors since 1811, when New York passed a law that soon was imitated by other states.

The Role of a Board

There are two factors that heavily influence the role of a board in any privately held company. Those are the status of ownership and the status of leadership within the organization. In general, the broader the ownership of the company in terms of number of owners, and the further from the first generation of leadership the company has traveled, the larger the probability that the board will be heavily populated by independent directors and actively involved in the affairs of the company on a strategic level.

These two factors—ownership and leadership status—often play a key role when owner-founder firms transition to organizations owned by employees and led by professional managers. In founder-owned companies, boards are often passive and populated by family and close associates. Another frequent option chosen by founder-owners is the advisory board, which has no legal status and authority but may have considerable influence on the leader. As ownership becomes less concentrated and the founder transitions out of leadership, boards may over time become more active and independent. This tendency toward more active independent boards also is evident if owner-founder managed firms become publicly owned or are sold to investment groups.

Jack Veale, a consultant to privately held companies, has identified five types of board practice:

1. *The passive board:* The passive board may have few or no independent directors, and if they are present, they are probably trusted lawyers, accountants, or bankers who may not pass the common definition of "independent," due to their supplier relationship with the company.

This board will probably have a strong founding CEO who serves both the roles of CEO and chairman. The CEO calls the meetings of the board whenever he or she deems it necessary and controls the function and actions of the board. There is limited activity and participation by board members and limited accountability. The purpose of the board is principally to ratify management decisions and make them legal.

2. *The certifying board:* The certifying board is somewhat more active than the passive board. Its principal function is to certify to the shareholders that the CEO is performing according to expectations. This board has a great need for independent directors who are willing to change management if needed to be credible to the owners. In these boards, the CEO is likely to be evaluated by the external board members.

3. *The engaged board:* This board is easily more active than the previous two. It is heavily populated with outsiders who provide inside advice and support to the CEO and the management team. There is a high level of interaction and discussion at board meetings. The engaged board takes time to define the roles and responsibilities of board members and the boundaries and responsibilities of both the board and the CEO. An engaged board is likely to have several committees, such as the audit committee, the compensation committee, and the governance committee. This board understands it is ultimately responsible for oversight of the CEO and company performance as well as succession planning. This board will sometimes seek outside experts that can add value to its decision-making process.

4. *The intervening board:* An intervening board is usually found in a crisis situation such as an absent or dysfunctional CEO. It is characterized by frequent meetings on short notice and intense involvement with key crisis issues. The primary focus is on achieving action plans to correct the current situation.

5. *The operating board*: The operating board is also heavily populated by independent directors and is often found in start-up environments such as new companies or new divisions with outside financing. This group may make key decisions as a group that management then implements. The population of the group helps fill in manage-

ment experience gaps. The group tends to be hands-on, focusing on selected high-priority activities such as developing product market systems, staffing, or financing the organization.

According to the National Association of Corporate Directors, to be effective, any board must be made up of the right people who operate within a culture that emphasizes and promotes candid communication and rigorous decision-making. The group must set relevant strategic issues and focus on those that will help the company maximize its long-term value. In this environment, that board must be provided with the right information and have a robust process for making informed decisions and holding management accountable for results.

Within this context, the most important role of a board is to select the CEO and provide for leadership and development and succession processes for the CEO and the senior management team. In addition, there is legal foundation as well as historic precedent for the board performing an oversight function: Are promised results achieved? Are plans realized? Is the conduct of the company within established guidelines for agreed-upon ethics and principles? In addition to these questions, the board is often called upon to provide guidance to management decision-making. Here, the boundaries between board and CEO functions can sometimes be tested. However, the board does have a responsibility to transfer the experience of its members to those entrusted with making decisions on a contemporaneous basis. Increasingly, especially in companies with diverse ownership, the board is called on to oversee regulatory compliance. Historically, this meant working with the auditors on accurate financial statements, but more recently the role has been broadened to include compliance with government regulations, governance regulations, and legislation such as Sarbanes-Oxley. Finally, with increasing frequency, the board has played an active role in communications with shareholders. These communications may take place routinely at annual meetings and in quarterly reports, but they may also occur on special occasions such as CEO succession or major news events.

Over the past decade, boards have, by necessity, become much more activist, especially in companies where management and ownership are substantially separated. For example:

- There is a clear trend toward an increasing number of "independent" directors and a decreasing number of "insiders."
- As the incidence of management lapses, abuses, and fraud has increased, board committees have become more active and independent, and oversight has increased.
- In response to shareholder pressure, boards have become increasingly intolerant of poor performance by those who lead.

While these trends, and governmental effort to correct abuse through regulation, have been aimed primarily at public companies, the impact has often been clearly felt in the private company sector. As shareholder activism increases, board oversight will continue to increase in response.

Board Makeup

The appropriate makeup of the board is heavily dependent on which stages the board is in. For example, passive boards may be populated by a limited number of family members and trusted advisors who have economic relationships with the company. This may work fine in a situation where a strong CEO controls the board function and the ownership of the company. But as companies grow more diverse in their ownership and as management moves beyond the first generation, a strong case can be made for increasing the population of truly independent outside board members. Companies in such situations should give careful thought to the skills and experience needed on the board. Examples of high-priority skills include prior or present CEOs, considerable financial expertise outside the United States, knowledge of the industry, and experience in the marketplace or with the technology owned by the company. As a group, directors should thoroughly understand the company's business, industry, and competition. The board should be a source for quality ideas, contacts, and support for best practices. Board members should understand the development and execution of appropriate company strategies, and they should be able to establish high (and measurable) standards for senior management performance. Board members should provide a key support role in attracting a top leadership team and creatively linking management compensation to the creation of shareholder value. Thus, a good board member will have a variety of skills and experiences to bring to the board and a depth of experience that may not be present anywhere in the existing organization.

Good members insist on timely and accurate information necessary to make quality decisions. They also insist on honesty and forthrightness on the part of management. Good board members are willing do their homework, study issues in advance, and participate actively in board discussions, including the constructive use of dissent where appropriate. A fully engaged board can be a powerful influence in the focus on and achievement of worthy company goals.

Recruitment, Orientation, and Compensation

With some exceptions, board members for most companies can be found within a one- to two-hour drive from headquarters or another frequent meeting place. Exceptions might be someone who is particularly well steeped in the company's technology or has an unusual degree of industry knowledge. If the recruitment focus is local, it is probably best to shy away from social clubs and nonprofits in favor of referrals from existing board members; recommendations from local lawyers, accountants and bankers; and members of certain relevant organizations, such as a business and industry association, the National Association of Corporate Directors, or a member of the local World Affairs Council. Before any recruitment efforts, there should be a job description or profile written for each set of experiences desired on the board. Examples might include one for CEO experience, one for financial expertise, one for knowledge of the business processes (science, manufacturing technology, marketing strategies, and so on) of the company, and one for international experience. Such people should be in the stage of their careers where they are ready and willing give something back and have the time to do so.

As a general rule, it is advisable to have three to five candidates for each board member slot. This implies an initial screening process. The initial screenings can be done by comparing resumes submitted to job profiles. Here, the idea is looking for matches between a candidate's experience and the requirements of the job. Once the initial screening takes place, usually by a member of the governance committee, a series of interviews can begin with members of the committee or the committee as a whole. Once the committee has a slate for consideration by the full board, there should be an opportunity for the candidates to present themselves to the full board and for one-on-one interaction and evaluation. It is only after these efforts, which may go on for several months, that the board feels confident and comfortable to recommend a slate to shareholders.

Once members have been approved by the shareholders, it is necessary for maximum board effectiveness to conduct a thorough multimonth orientation program, which should involve such things as the reading of a year or more of past board minutes, the study of company product brochures, a thorough review of the financial statements with the CFO of the company, tours of the facilities, and interviews with members of senior management. Too often, board members are asked to give thoughtful advice and make informed decisions in the absence of a high-quality orientation program. If a high-quality program is implemented, a "catch as catch can" three-year orientation process can be accomplished in three months with obvious benefit to the company, its shareholders, and senior management.

Compensation matters can be a thorny issue, especially in private companies. While board member compensation is a matter of public record in public companies, private companies have no obligation to disclose this information and often decline to do so. Two general rules seem to apply: the larger the company the higher the compensation, and the higher the risk (as in public companies) the higher the compensation. As a starting point, one might consider using data from the annual National Association of Corporate Directors compensation surveys for public companies, and the biannual survey of compensation and activity and governance activity in private companies. The compensation in public companies should probably be viewed as an upper boundary by private companies since some level of discount factor applies due to the increased risk of serving on a public company board. Chapter 8 of this book ("ESOP Corporate Governance in a New Era") has a survey of ESOP companies concerning board compensation practices.

The Evolution of the Board at Reflexite Corporation from 1970 to the Present

My company, Reflexite Corporation, was founded in 1970 by two brothers and their brother-in-law. In the early days, the board consisted of the three owners, and they met only when necessary to fulfill legal requirements. However, things changed in 1977 when they sold 25% of Reflexite to a customer company and 10% to two employees. At that point, the board was expanded from three to eight members: the original three, two representatives from the customer company, the company's banker and lawyer, and a local business executive who was a good friend of the founding brothers. The result was that a 25% owner also had 25% of the board seats. This board met from two to four times per year. At the request of the founders and the company lawyer, the meetings were informal, as reflected in the brief meeting notes of that era.

In 1983, when the brothers were in their mid-60s, a successor president (myself) was hired from outside the company and elected to the board, and discussions about the future ownership of the company became a frequent topic at board meetings.

In 1985, the founders and I decided to transition significant ownership to an ESOP, and I requested support for building a stronger, more involved outside board of directors to provide appropriate guidance and oversight. With the first ESOP transaction, the number of owners expanded from 5 to 85, and the lawyer, banker, and friend were replaced by local businesspeople with no connection to the company other than their membership on the board. The Reflexite board evolved from a small group meeting minimum legal requirements to a fully functioning board with three committees and eight members as the company evolved from its birth in 1970 to $10 million in sales and 100 employee-owners in 1990. The evolution continued as the company reached its current size (as of 2009) of $80 million in sales and 450 employee-owners.

In 2006, one third of the company was sold by long-term investors to an outside institutional investment company. As a result, the board was expanded from eight to eleven members to achieve an equitable balance of membership interests. There is general agreement that the number should be reduced over time toward seven to eight. Members have diverse experience and expertise, as shown in table 9-1.

The Role of the Board in ESOP Companies 105

Table 9-1. Experience of Reflexite Board Members

Type of Experience	Number of Reflexite Board Members with Such Experience
CEO	4
CFO	3
Technology	2
Corporation finance/transactions	2
International business	6

Because some of the members have more than one area of expertise, the total exceeds eleven. Of the eleven members, two are insiders and nine are outsiders. The board meets four to six times per year.

There are four board committees:

1. *The executive committee.* Consists of the chairman and two other board members to act for the full board in emergencies. It has not met in the past decade because the board has a preference for full board meetings whenever possible.

2. *The compensation committee.* Responsible for determining the compensation for the board, the CEO, and his direct reports. Also responsible for broad-based equity compensation (ESOP, options, ESPP) and cash bonus systems. It meets four to six times per year.

3. *The audit and finance committee.* Responsible for the annual certified audit, ethics policies, capital structure, and financial projections. It meets three to five times per year.

4. *The governance committee.* Responsible for governance issues, such as committee structure, compliance with regulatory requirements, determination of management vs. board responsibilities, and nominations to the board. It meets two to three times per year.

In addition, there are three business unit advisory boards, which provide advice and counsel to the leadership of the company's three business units. There are composed of both outside board members and members of senior management. Meetings are held approximately twice per year.

In large measure, the high level of board activity results from three major changes taking place within the company: a change in business strategy, a CEO succession, and a change in ownership. There is an expectation that the level of activity will decline as these changes are successfully implemented.

Conclusion

The Reflexite board is more institutionalized and more developed than most boards in ESOP companies. As the survey in the chapter 8 of this book shows, while many ESOP companies are moving toward more formal board structures, informal boards, made up largely of insiders, remain the norm. In my experience, however, the investment of time and money in our board has been an excellent investment, helping the company prosper and maintaining a high level of credibility with our employee owners and outside owners.

About the Authors

Merri E. Ash has been in the employee benefits field for over 35 years. She joined First Bankers Trust Services, Inc. (FBTS) in 2002 as a trust officer and the director of marketing and was promoted to vice president in 2006. FBTS serves as the ESOP trustee for over 200 employee-owned companies. Merri has served as the benefits manager for the Jonathan Corporation of Norfolk, Virginia, an employee-owned company, and has written many articles on administering ESOPs while serving as chairperson of the ESOP Association's Administrative Advisory Committee. Merri also serves on the board of governors of the ESOP Association and is on the board of trustees of the Employee Ownership Foundation.

Kelly Q. Driscoll is senior managing director of State Street Global Advisors Asia Limited. She is responsible for all of State Street's investment management activities in Asia, excluding Japan. Before joining SSgA Asia, she was senior managing director of the Fiduciary Group of SSgA in the United States. Since joining State Street in 1982, Kelly has served in various roles specializing in legal, fiduciary and investment management. Kelly holds an LLM in banking law from Boston University School of Law, a JD from Suffolk University Law School, and a BA from Catholic University.

Michael G. Falk is a senior manager in the Employee Benefits Tax practice at Deloitte & Touche, LLP. Mr. Falk specializes in ERISA and qualified retirement plans, executive compensation plans, and equity arrangements. He received a JD, magna cum laude, from the University of Illinois College of Law and a BA from Northwestern University. Before joining Deloitte, he practiced law with the Employee Benefits group of McDermott, Will & Emery.

Colleen Helmer is a senior manager in Deloitte & Touche's Employee Benefits Tax practice. Colleen has responsibility for the Sarbanes-Oxley Section 404 activities related to employee benefits in Deloitte's Chicago office and has assisted on Sarbanes-Oxley-related projects for clients in the insurance and financial services industries. Before joining Deloitte, she practiced law with the Employee Benefits group of Sidley Austin Brown & Wood. Colleen received a JD from John Marshall Law School and a B.A. from Valparaiso University.

Brian Ippensen is the president of First Bankers Trust Services, Inc. (FBTS). FBTS is a nationally recognized trust provider to ESOPs in over 37 states. Mr. Ippensen coordinates the staff personnel involved in employee benefits, personal trust, corporate trust, and individual retirement accounts. Before joining FBTS, Mr. Ippensen was employed by McGladrey & Pullen's audit and tax group. While there, he assisted with and managed audits of agricultural businesses, financial institutions, health and welfare plans, and retirement plans. He is a member of the ESOP Association's Fiduciary Committee and has spoken at ESOP Association and NCEO national and local conferences. Mr. Ippensen is a certified public accountant and a certified managerial accountant.

Alex W. Kirby was a student at Canisius College when he coauthored his chapter in this book. He spent the summer before his final undergraduate year as an intern in the Fiduciary Group at State Street Global Advisors in Boston, MA, where he coauthored several ERISA fiduciary articles. Alex was one of only 10 undergraduates selected to the student-managed Golden Griffin Equity fund at Canisius College, managing over a half-million dollars.

About the Authors

Anthony Mathews is the director of the Beyster Institute at the Rady School of Management at the University of California, San Diego. He joined the Beyster Institute, which promotes employee ownership, after retiring from a nearly 30-year-long career as one of the best-known ESOP and employee ownership experts in the U.S. Before his retirement, Tony served as a vice president and senior consultant with Principal Financial Group. He is a frequent speaker and author on a wide range of employee ownership issues. He is a founding member of the Administrative Advisory Committee of the ESOP Association (TEA) and a former director of TEA. He is also a member of the steering committee of TEA's Western States chapter. He is a former chair of the board of directors of the National Center for Employee Ownership (NCEO) and has been a member of many other associations with interests in employee ownership, pensions, and related matters. Tony also serves as an independent outside director for several employee ownership companies in California. He received his BA from Loyola University of Los Angeles in 1971 and his MA from UCLA in 1976.

Helen H. Morrison is with the Office of Tax Policy in the Treasury Department in Washington D.C. When she wrote her chapters in this book, she was a principal at Deloitte & Touche and the national practice leader for the ESOP Advisory Services practice group. She has authored or coauthored several articles and books on ESOPs and executive compensation. She has been an adjunct professor of employee benefits and executive compensation at John Marshall Law School's Master of Tax program and a frequent speaker at ESOP conferences, including those of the NCEO. Before joining Deloitte & Touche, Ms. Morrison was a partner in the Employee Benefits group at McDermott, Will & Emery. She received her bachelor's degree in 1979 from Trinity College, Hartford, CT, and her JD degree, cum laude, in 1985 from Illinois Institute of Technology/Chicago-Kent College of Law.

Corey Rosen is the executive director and cofounder of the National Center for Employee Ownership (NCEO), a private, nonprofit membership, information, and research organization in Oakland, CA. The NCEO is widely considered to be the authoritative source on broad-based employee ownership plans. He cofounded the NCEO in 1981 after working for five years as a professional staff member in the U.S. Senate, where he helped draft legislation on employee ownership plans. Before that, he taught political science at Ripon College. He is the author or coauthor of many books and over 100 articles on employee ownership, and coauthor (with John Case and Martin Staubus) of *Equity: Why Employee Ownership Is Good for Business* (Harvard Business School Press, 2005). He was the subject of an extensive interview in *Inc.* magazine in August 2000; has appeared frequently on CNN, PBS, NPR, and other network programs; and is regularly quoted in the *Wall Street Journal,* the *New York Times,* and other leading publications. He has a PhD in political science from Cornell University and serves on the advisory board of the Certified Equity Professional Institute.

James Steiker, founder, chairman, and CEO of SES Advisors, Inc., has more than 25 years of experience with focusing on ESOP and employee ownership matters as a legal and financial advisor. Jim is a member of the NCEO's board of directors, is a trustee of the Employee Ownership Foundation and a member of the ESOP Association's Finance Committee, and serves on the boards of many ESOP companies. He is a frequent speaker on ESOP matters and a regular contributor to the *Journal of Employee Ownership Law and Finance.*

Cecil Ursprung is the executive chairman and former CEO of Reflexite Corporation, an employee-owned manufacturer of plastic optical films and components. He has been employed at Reflexite since 1983. His past experience includes marketing and management positions with Marketing Displays, Inc., Container Corporation of America, and Anheuser Busch. His education includes a degree in economics and finance from Baylor University, an MBA from Washington University in St. Louis, and postgraduate work at the University of Michigan. Ursprung has served on the advisory boards of four corporations, ranging from a startup to one with $40 million in sales, and two nonprofit organizations. He is currently on the board of directors of Lewis Tree Service, Inc., a 2,600-employee ESOP company, and Dynasil Corporation, a public company in the photonics market. In 1992, he and the employee-owners of Reflexite were chosen as *Inc.* magazine's Entrepreneurs of the Year.

About the NCEO

The National Center for Employee Ownership (NCEO) is widely considered to be the leading authority in employee ownership in the U.S. and the world. Established in 1981 as a nonprofit information and membership organization, it now has over 2,500 members, including companies, professionals, unions, government officials, academics, and interested individuals. It is funded entirely through the work it does.

The NCEO's mission is to provide the most objective, reliable information possible about employee ownership at the most affordable price possible. As part of the NCEO's commitment to providing objective information, it does not lobby or provide ongoing consulting services. The NCEO publishes a variety of materials on employee ownership and participation, provides online education, and holds dozens of seminars, Webinars, and conferences on employee ownership annually. The NCEO's work includes extensive contacts with the media, both through articles written for trade and professional publications and through interviews with reporters. It has written or edited five books for outside publishers during the past two decades. Finally, the NCEO maintains an extensive Web site at www.nceo.org.

See the following page for information on membership benefits and fees. To join, see the order form at the end of this section, visit our Web site at www.nceo.org, or telephone us at 510-208-1300.

Membership Benefits

NCEO members receive the following benefits:

- The bimonthly newsletter, *Employee Ownership Report,* which covers ESOPs, stock options, and employee participation.
- Access to the members-only area of the NCEO's Web site, which includes a searchable database of well over 200 NCEO members who are service providers in this field.
- Substantial discounts on publications and events produced by the NCEO (such as this book).
- Free access to live Webinars and conference calls.
- The right to telephone the NCEO for answers to general or specific questions regarding employee ownership.

An introductory NCEO membership costs $90 for one year ($100 outside the U.S.) and covers an entire company at all locations, a single office of a firm offering professional services in this field, or an individual with a business interest in employee ownership. Full-time students and faculty members who are not employed in the business sector may join at the academic rate of $40 for one year ($50 outside the U.S.).

Selected NCEO Publications

The NCEO offers a variety of publications on all aspects of employee ownership and participation. Following are descriptions of a few of our main publications. We publish new books and revise old ones on a yearly basis. To obtain the most current information on what we have available, visit our extensive Web site at www.nceo.org or call us at 510-208-1300.

Employee Stock Ownership Plans (ESOPs)

- *Understanding ESOPs* is an overview of the issues involved in establishing and operating an ESOP.

    $25 for NCEO members, $35 for nonmembers

- *S Corporation ESOPs* introduces the reader to how ESOPs work and then discusses the legal, valuation, administrative, and other issues associated with S corporation ESOPs.

    $25 for NCEO members, $35 for nonmembers

- *ESOP Valuation* brings together and updates where needed the best articles on ESOP valuation we have published in our journal.

    $25 for NCEO members, $35 for nonmembers

- *The ESOP Company Board Handbook* is a guide for board members in ESOP companies.

    $25 for NCEO members, $35 for nonmembers

- The *ESOP Company Board Member Training Package* combines *The ESOP Company Board Handbook* with two prerecorded Webinars.

    $50 for NCEO members, $75 for nonmembers

- *Executive Compensation in ESOP Companies* discusses executive compensation issues, special ESOP considerations, and a survey of executive compensation in ESOP companies.

    $25 for NCEO members, $35 for nonmembers

- *The Inside ESOP Fiduciary Handbook* provides an overview of the issues involved in being a fiduciary at an ESOP company.

    $10 for NCEO members, $15 for nonmembers

- *How ESOP Companies Handle the Repurchase Obligation* has essays and recent research on the subject.

    $25 for NCEO members, $35 for nonmembers

- *ESOPs and Corporate Governance* covers everything from shareholder rights to the impact of Sarbanes-Oxley to choosing a fiduciary.

    $25 for NCEO members, $35 for nonmembers

- *Selling to an ESOP* is a guide for owners, managers, and advisors of closely held businesses, with a particular focus on the tax-deferred Section 1042 "rollover" for C corporation owners.

    $25 for NCEO members, $35 for nonmembers

- *Model ESOP* provides a sample ESOP plan, with alternative provisions given to tailor the plan to individual needs. It also includes a section-by-section explanation of the plan and other supporting materials.

    $50 for NCEO members, $75 for nonmembers

- *Administrative Issues for ESOP Companies* is a guide to the issues that arise in operating an ESOP, from filing Form 5500 to dealing with Internal Revenue Service or Department of Labor audits.

    $25 for NCEO members, $35 for nonmembers

- *The ESOP Communications Sourcebook* provides ideas for and examples of communicating an ESOP to employees and customers. It includes a CD with communications materials, including many documents that readers can customize for their own companies.

    $35 for NCEO members, $50 for nonmembers

Equity Compensation

- *The Decision-Maker's Guide to Equity Compensation* describes the various types of equity compensation, how they work, and how to decide how much to give and to whom.

    $35 for NCEO members, $50 for nonmembers

- *Beyond Stock Options* is a complete guide, including annotated model plans, to phantom stock, restricted stock, stock appreciation rights, performance awards, etc. Includes a CD with plan documents.

    $35 for NCEO members, $50 for nonmembers

- *The Stock Options Book* is a straightforward, comprehensive overview covering the legal, accounting, regulatory, and design issues involved in implementing a stock option or stock purchase plan.

    $25 for NCEO members, $35 for nonmembers

- *Equity Compensation for Limited Liability Companies* describes how equity compensation works in an LLC and provides a model plan document (which is included on an accompanying CD).

    $25 for NCEO members, $35 for nonmembers

About the NCEO

- *Equity-Based Compensation for Multinational Corporations* describes how companies can use stock options and other equity-based programs across the world. It includes a country-by-country summary of tax and legal issues as well as a detailed case study.

    $25 for NCEO members, $35 for nonmembers

Employee Involvement and Management

- *The Ownership Edge* is a handbook for engaging the full entrepreneurial potential of a employee-owned company's workforce through education, information, and engagement.

    $25 for NCEO members, $35 for nonmembers

- *Front Line Finance* gives step-by-step instructions for teaching business literacy, emphasizing ESOPs.

    $50 for NCEO members, $75 for nonmembers

Other

- *Section 401(k) Plans and Employee Ownership* focuses on how company stock is used in 401(k) plans, both in stand-alone 401(k) plans and combination 401(k)-ESOP plans ("KSOPs").

    $25 for NCEO members, $35 for nonmembers

- *The Journal of Employee Ownership Law and Finance* is the only professional journal solely devoted to employee ownership. Articles are written by leading experts and cover ESOPs, stock options, and related subjects in depth.

    One-year subscription (four issues):
    $75 for NCEO members, $100 for nonmembers

To join the NCEO as a member or to order any of the publications listed on the preceding pages, use the order form on the following page, use the secure ordering system on our Web site at www.nceo.org, or call us at 510-208-1300. If you join at the same time you order publications, you will receive the members-only publication discounts.

Order Form

To order, fill out this form and mail it with your credit card information or check to the NCEO at 1736 Franklin St., 8th Flr., Oakland, CA 94612; fax it with your credit card information to the NCEO at 510-272-9510; telephone us at 510-208-1300 with your credit card in hand; or order at our Web site, www.nceo.org. If you are not already a member, you can join now to receive member discounts on any publications you order.

Name

Organization

Address

City, State, Zip (Country)

Telephone   Fax   E-mail

Method of Payment: ❑ Check (payable to "NCEO")   ❑ Visa   ❑ M/C   ❑ AMEX

Credit Card Number

Signature   Exp. Date

Checks are accepted only for orders from the U.S. and must be in U.S. currency.

Title	Qty.	Price	Total

Tax: California residents add 9.75% sales tax (on publications only, not membership or Journal subscriptions)

Shipping: In the U.S , first publication $5, each add'l $1; elsewhere, we charge exact shipping costs to your credit card, plus a $10 handling surcharge; no shipping charges for membership or Journal subscriptions

Introductory NCEO Membership: $90 for one year ($100 outside the U.S.)

Subtotal	$
Sales Tax	$
Shipping	$
Membership	$
TOTAL DUE	$